The Experts Say "Yes!" to
Does Jane Compute?

"Just what we need to make sure we don't have to play the same catch-up game with girls and computers that we did with girls and sports. Helpful, accessible, and informative, a must-read for parents, teachers—or, in fact, anyone concerned with our daughters' futures."

—Joan Ryan, author of *Little Girls in Pretty Boxes*

"This book will help awaken American families to the role they can play in encouraging their daughters' involvement in cybersapce."

—Carolyn L. Kennedy, director, Special Projects,
Girl Scouts of America

ROBERTA FURGER is a contributing editor for *PC World*, America's largest monthly computer magazine. Her articles have appeared in *Newsweek*, *Child*, *Parenting*, the *San Francisco Examiner*, *Web* magazine, and *Family Circle's Computers Made Easy*. She spearheaded *PC World*'s first extended coverage of children's software, including a special report, "Smart Computing for Kids," published jointly by *PC World* and *Child Magazine*. She lives with her husband and two young children in the San Francisco Bay area.

Does Jane Compute?

Preserving Our Daughters' Place in the Cyber Revolution

Roberta Furger

WARNER BOOKS

A Time Warner Company

#36877518

Warner Books, Inc., 1271 Avenue of the Americas, New York, NY 10020

Visit our Web site at
http://warnerbooks.com

68272

 A Time Warner Company

Printed in the United States of America
First Printing: February 1998
10 9 8 7 6 5 4 3 2 1

HQ
777
.F87
1998

Library of Congress Cataloging-in-Publication Data

Furger, Roberta.
  Does Jane compute? : preserving our daughters' place in the cyber revolution / Roberta Furger.
    p. cm.
  ISBN 0-446-67311-0
  1. Girls—Computer network resources.   2. Girls—Education.
  3. Computers—Study and teaching.   4. Sexism in education.
  I. Title.
  HQ777.F87 1998
  004'.083'42—dc21   97-20837
                                                          CIP

Cover design by Robin Loc Monda
Cover photo by James Levine/FPG
Book design and text composition by Ralph L. Fowler

*This book is dedicated to
my husband, Gary,
and my two children,
Jessie and Michael*

Acknowledgments

Although mine is the only name that appears on the cover, this book would never have been written without the help and support of many friends and colleagues.

Jennie McDonald provided the initial spark that set this project into motion and has been a constant source of encouragement, advice, and friendship along the way. My editor at Warner Books, Caryn Karmatz Rudy, deftly shaped and guided the book with her patience, thoughtful editorial advice, and encouraging words. Thank you, Caryn.

To my friends who read the manuscript: Bronwyn Fryer, Lauren Black, and Meredith Steiner, thank you for your honest comments and thoughtful suggestions. I am particularly grateful to Christina Spence, who read chapters as I churned them out, listened to my ramblings, and was always there with a voice of reason and a cup of coffee. Thanks, also to my friends and colleagues at *PC World*, who for several months put up with one very pre-occupied columnist.

While researching this book, I was fortunate to meet and speak with dozens of bright young women, who shared with me their accomplishments and their frustrations—both on the computer and off. I also had the pleasure of speaking with many of their parents, teachers, and mentors who graciously answered my questions and shared their thoughts and concerns. I would also like to acknowledge Dr. Maria Klawe, Jo Sanders, and Dr. Anita Borg whose work has inspired me and who have given so generously of their time.

My friends and family were terrific during the writing of this book. In particular, I'd like to thank my sister Mo, who was always there for me; Christina, who shared her mom with Jessie and Michael; Lisa and Debbie for the coffee breaks, puppy sitting, and eleventh-hour assistance; Jack and Shirley Kershner, who let my husband and children invade their home every weekend so I could write in peace and quiet; and my mother, Carmel Furger, for her love and support.

I am blessed with a truly amazing family. My children, Jessie and Michael, were my inspiration throughout the writing of this book. They encouraged me when I was tired, celebrated with me the completion of each chapter, and even offered suggestions when I was stymied.

Lastly, thank you to Gary Kershner, my husband, friend, and partner, who held everything together and kept us all relatively sane while I wrote. I would never have made it through this project without his unfailing support, encouragement, and love.

Contents

Author's Note

Does Jane Compute?

In the 1970s, the nation became obsessed with boys' low verbal scores on standardized tests. The question, "Why can't Johnny read?" became a rallying cry for parents and teachers, prompting a complete rethinking of the way verbal and reading skills were taught in school.

It's time to ask a new question, to marshal our resources to face a new challenge, one that, like Johnny's low verbal scores, affects half the children in the United States. Individually and collectively, we need to ask, "Does Jane compute?" None of us should be satisfied until the answer for each of our daughters is a resounding, unequivocal, enthusiastic *yes*.

Introduction

It was a hot August afternoon and computer camp activities were beginning to wind down for the day. I'd just spent the last several hours talking to six teenage girls who, along with forty-eight boys, were learning programming tips and tricks at the week-long camp in Cambridge, Massachusetts. We'd talked about why they came to camp, what interested them about computers, and about how they felt about being part of such a distinct minority that week. As I was getting ready to leave, two of the girls pulled me aside and asked if I could stay for a few more minutes. "We want to talk to you about something," one said eagerly. As we plopped ourselves down on the couches outside the computer room, the girls proceeded to fill me in on the facts of life—computer life, that is.

Over the course of the day, some of the girls had been eager to talk, sharing with me everything from details about programs they'd participated in at their schools to their thoughts on coed versus single-sex computer camps and classes. A few, though, had been considerably more cautious, wondering, it seemed, if they could really trust this *thirtysomething* woman they'd just met. I couldn't help but feel as if I'd passed some sort of test when they pulled me aside to talk.

"Okay, it's like this," explained Margaret S., a fourteen-year-old who spoke to me in the way a parent might explain a complicated issue to a young child. "I know guys at my school who are pretty smart and who are really into computers. For them, that's okay. But when a girl knows a lot about computers, that's not good. Sure girls like games. They just don't talk about it. That wouldn't be cool."

Margaret's smart, well-rounded, and has clearly given some thought to the subject of girls and computers. She'd just finished telling me how important computers are to her future. She decided to go to this camp when most of her friends were off swimming or taking riding lessons because she wanted to learn more about the technology (though having a week away from home also played a role in her decision). So, if being good at computers, even taking an interest in them is so uncool, I wondered, how had Margaret managed to come to a computer camp without risking being labeled some kind of nerd or geek? "I didn't talk about it much," she said casually. "The only people I told that I was going to a computer camp were the friends whose parents were in the computer business. I haven't told anyone else. They just wouldn't understand the point."

Margaret wasn't the only closet computer camper I met that summer. Across the country on the Stanford University campus, thirteen-year-old Susan A. had an even stronger reaction when I asked another group of girls what their friends thought about their stay at computer camp. "Tell my friends? No way," she said, practically shuddering at the thought. "They'd think I was nerdy. They'd disown me."

Were Margaret and Susan exaggerating the effects of peer pressure for my benefit? I don't think so. These girls, like so many of the preteen and teenage girls I would interview over the next nine months, understood the unwritten yet incredibly powerful rule about computers: girls could use them for school, they could send e-mail, chat, or play games now and then, but only guys could be *into* computers, only guys could be really good at them. No one has to explain the rules to these girls—they've grown up learning about them through the subtle, and not-so-subtle, ways in which our society encourages boys to explore all things technical, while guiding girls away from these activities.

Elizabeth Debold, a member of the Harvard Project, an ongoing study on adolescent girls, explains it this way: "When girls get to junior high and high school . . . [they] find themselves walking a very thin line, trying to figure out what they need to do to be okay. Many girls become afraid to engage in technology, math, or science. It's too risky to take [those subjects] on."[1]

That's not to say that every girl becomes disinterested in computers when she reaches adolescence. Some girls, such as Margaret, are aware of the pressures, yet pursue their interests anyway. They become expert Web page designers, talented programmers, even skilled gamers. But there are many more who don't engage in computers. There are many more for whom this unwritten rule becomes an impediment to exploration, to discovery, and ultimately, to the competence and the confidence that are critical for anyone—male or female—living in such a technologically driven age.

I didn't grow up with personal computers. I was out of college and working at my third job as a writer and reporter before I sat down and flipped the "on" switch for the first time. I had exaggerated my knowledge of PCs *just a tad* to get a position writing and editing corporate newsletters for businesses who hadn't yet ventured into the world of desktop publishing. After just one week on the job I found myself sitting in front of an IBM PC with an issue to get out and absolutely no idea what to do. Now, twelve years and many, many hours of computing time later, I still remember the sense of panic, of helplessness, and of frustration as I first stared at the intimidating blank screen.

It took a long time before I felt at home in front of a computer. For years I limited my use to word processing, the tool of my trade. I didn't explore new applications— or even the more advanced features of the software I used every day. Then gradually, I began to investigate other uses: spreadsheets and databases for work, budgeting software for home, online services for work and for fun. It took a long time, though, before I was able to approach a new application or a new hardware device with confidence and ease.

Maybe that's why I am in such awe of my daughter. At eight years old, she is as comfortable installing a new software program as she is putting a tape in the VCR. She's confident, at times even cocky, about her abilities and readily challenges anyone in the house to try to break her record high score on her favorite arcade game. She is proud of her prowess, yet she takes her participation for granted. It simply does not occur to her to think of approaching computers any other way. I marvel at her confidence and praise her for each day's accomplishments, but I can't help but wonder where she'll be two, four, or six years from now. Will she, like so many of the girls I met, find herself trying to reconcile her own interests with the expectations of her peers and the larger society? Or will she continue to enjoy the fun, the challenge, the excitement of exploring new technological activities?

Although right now my children view the computer

as a toy, you only have to look around to see it is much more than that. The personal computer has changed the way we spend our free time and the way we work.

For households with access to the Internet or an online service, computers are changing the way we stay in touch with family and friends. Parents send e-mail to their children away at college. Girls and boys find keypals (electronic penpals) in faraway places. We can send e-mail to everyone from rock stars to politicians (though there's no guarantee that any of them will write back). Although the hype about the World Wide Web is still far ahead of the reality, we can now go online to bank, shop, even find out the latest word on the chicken pox vaccine. Through e-mail, chats, and personal Web pages, moms and dads, sons and daughters are sharing their views and opinions with people across town and around the world.

Everyone—boys and girls, men and women—need to participate in these changes if they are to be productive members of society. And yet, everyone isn't participating. Not all of our daughters are participating. They don't log on as often as boys, they don't play games, join computer clubs, or take advanced classes as often as boys. And when they get older, they don't pursue careers in technical fields as often as men.

Comparisons are frequently made between girls' perceived disinterest in computers and their disinterest in math and science. Others liken computers to sports, because both remain the domain of men and boys. Both comparisons come close, but neither really hits the mark. As critical as high-level math and science courses can be in determining a young girl's future, the chances of actually *using* calculus in life are pretty slim. And while playing a sport and enjoying the thrill of competing can have a tremendous effect on a young girl's confidence and her willingness to take on challenges, our daughters aren't going to need to know how to make a double play, or how to dribble the soccer ball down the field for a fast break, in order to be productive adults.

The same can't be said of computers. Our children will need well-honed computer skills for so many aspects of their adult lives. A base level of computer skills is assumed for incoming college freshmen and has become a necessity in many trades and professions. By the year 2000, sixty percent of all new jobs will require computer competence.[2] High-tech jobs are among the fastest-growing (and best-paid) positions, according to the Bureau of Labor Statistics.[3] And just about every job—from accountant to lawyer, from biologist to architect—will depend on sophisticated computer skills.

In the coming pages, you'll read about young women who are staking their claim on the digital frontier. You'll meet girls who at home and at school are gaining the skills they'll need to thrive in the twenty-first century. (Although most of the girls and young women are identified by their real names, some names have been changed to protect an individual's privacy.) You'll also meet teachers, parents, and concerned adults who are encouraging and supporting their efforts every step of the way.

But as I spoke with girls about their achievements, time and again a disturbing trend emerged: many young women shared a nagging insecurity about their facility for computers. They kept their accomplishments to themselves, or only shared them with friends they met online. They downplayed their achievements, so as not to call attention to themselves.

The difference between boys and girls in this area is dramatic. Take twelve-year-old James, for example, a boy at one of the schools I visited. As I was hanging out at the computer lab waiting for the next class to come in he sauntered up to me and announced, "Everyone thinks of me as a computer nerd," clearly proud of the distinction. In contrast, girls who were just as talented were embarrassed by any recognition. Fifteen-year-old Cindy T. taught herself Java, a complex programming language for creating applications on the World Wide Web. She's also mastered several professional-level graphics packages. But when I praised her accomplishments, she only shrugged her shoulders and said, "My brother's better."

Although Cindy is far more computer savvy than many girls her age, her lack of confidence may keep her from pursuing computer technology as far as she might— as far as a boy would. In its 1992 report, *How Schools Shortchange Girls*, the American Association of University Women (AAUW) documents the strong correlation

between a girl's confidence in her abilities and a contin-
uation in math and science. Although males typically
drop out of these fields because they can't do the work,
females drop out *despite* their abilities.[4] In computer-
related fields, where men far outnumber women at both
the collegiate and professional level, confidence is just as
critical to a woman's success as competence.

The same invisible hand that pushes young women
away from math and science also pushes them away from
computers—or causes them to doubt their abilities. The
consequences are dramatic and far reaching. Every time
a teacher defers to a boy for computer assistance, every
time a parent puts the computer in the son's room, we
are telling our daughters that computers aren't really for
them. We're sowing seeds of doubt when we should be
providing support and encouragement.

For my daughter, the computer is no more a "boy
thing" than books or baseball or baby dolls. But my
daughter hasn't reached adolescence, when the ground
rules for girls suddenly change, when activities that were
once considered acceptable are suddenly inappropriate,
when computers—like math, sports, or science—become one more area that the guys get to master and claim
as their own.

I come to this subject not as a sociologist or an edu-
cator, but as a mother and as someone who has spent the
last ten years immersed in the fast-paced, male-oriented
world of the computer industry. As a writer and editor

I've covered everything from the latest hardware and software products to online shopping, but I've always shied away from the more technical approaches to stories, leaving those to my colleagues to write. One reason for this choice is that I am much more interested in how we can benefit from a new technology than I am in how it works. But I also wonder to what degree my penchant for the "softer stories" stems from insecurities about my technical competence—a fear of getting in over my head. Like so many of the girls I met, perhaps I, too, have shortchanged my own computer skills and knowledge—even after years of "proving" them to myself and others.

Will my daughter be stymied by the same insecurities? At eight, she has to be pried away from the computer. Will she gradually lose interest—and consciously or unconsciously come to think of computers as toys for men and boys? How can I encourage her to explore all the possibilities? What can I do to make sure both my son and my daughter are exposed to a wide range of material, and that they both have the opportunity to explore this powerful technology to whatever extent they choose?

In writing this book, I hope to answer those questions for myself, and the millions of other adults with girls and young women in their lives. And in doing so, to better prepare all of our daughters for life in the nineties and beyond.

Part 1: Jane@Home

1

Whose Computer Is It, Anyway?

When Suzy K. was in elementary school, she and her best friend both had Apple II GS computers. They loved to play games and their dads shared and nourished their fascination with the technology. Most Saturdays, Suzy and her dad would pack up their latest games and head over to her friend's house. The girls would play for hours while their fathers talked. It was a ritual that today both father and daughter remember fondly. A ritual that laid the groundwork for the years and accomplishments to come.

Suzy's family got their first computer when she was just five. They upgraded when she was seven, and again when she was nine. At eleven, Suzy had her own computer. At twelve she was an online regular. By the time I met Suzy, she was fourteen years old and managing an online forum for youth and teens in the San Francisco Bay Area on America Online, the country's largest online service.

Suzy is poised and confident, ready and willing to take on any challenge. She edited her middle school newspaper, ran for class president, even took up the guitar with the hopes of forming her own band. When it comes to computers, Suzy has no patience for those who think girls are somehow inherently less interested or less skilled than boys. "It's always been an equal thing for me," she says, slightly irritated that anyone might suggest otherwise.

Suzy is amazing. Her journey from curious little girl to confident, knowledgeable young woman leaves one wanting to believe, as she says, that there's "no difference between boys and girls when it comes to computers."

But Suzy's story is not every girl's story.

For one thing, Suzy's economic advantages set her apart. Few households had joined the computer revolution in 1987, when Suzy's family bought its first computer; fewer still are able to upgrade regularly to stay abreast of the technology. But it took more than a succession of new computers to get Suzy where she is today. It took the support of her parents, particularly as she made her way through the minefields of adolescence. The encouragement—and opportunities—have paid off. It wouldn't even occur to Suzy to think of computers as toys for boys. For years computers have been a source of fun and learning for her, and she can't imagine it any other way.

Suzy's parents never forced her to pursue an interest in computers, but they always made it possible for her to do so. They created an environment in which she could excel and thrive at an age when so many young girls start to doubt themselves and their abilities. Suzy's dad was particularly instrumental in her computer education. If his daughter tired of an activity, he would suggest another to revive her waning interests. When games got boring, he encouraged her to try programming; when Apple launched its online service, he signed her up as a tester; and when Suzy wanted to start her own youth forum online, her dad helped her formulate the proposal and get it to the right people.

Suzy's story *isn't* every girl's story, but it's not because other girls aren't interested in computers. Many are. What makes Suzy's story unique is that she was given the opportunity to discover her talents, to explore new areas. Many girls never get that chance. Too often, there's no one encouraging them to go for it, no one helping them to believe—to *know*—that they can.

On the Outside Looking In

Forty percent of all U.S. households with children now own a personal computer,[5] but having a computer in the home doesn't guarantee that everyone will get to use it. Homes such as Suzy's, in which a girl is the primary computer user, certainly exist. But they are not the norm. All too often girls find themselves on the fringe, watching and waiting for a turn as the men and the boys of the house stake their claim on the family computer.

Consider thirteen-year-old Patti R., for example, who lives in a small, affluent West Coast town. Her parents sent her to a two-week computer camp, but she rarely has a chance to use the computer at home. "My two brothers use it all day, every day," she explains, with a look that lets you know there's no point fighting for a turn. Although her brothers are frequent online users, the only opportunity Patti has had to explore the Internet was at computer camp. She'd found one game she enjoyed playing, but her brother removed it from the computer when he "needed more space for his stuff."

Patti isn't unique. In conversation after conversation, girls refer to the computer in their house as their "brother's computer" or their "father's computer." They talk about having to get their brother's permission before using the computer, or having to wait until their brother is done with "his stuff" (somehow more important) before they can get a turn.

Jo Sanders, a gender equity specialist, has heard it all before. For almost twenty years she has been offering workshops for parents, advising them on strategies for encouraging their daughters' computer use. After every talk, at least one mother (interestingly, it's usually the moms who attend her seminars) comes up to her with a look of chagrin on her face and says, "You know, I never thought about it before, but I guess I shouldn't keep the computer in my son's room."

Sometimes all it takes is recognition that they are encouraging gender-biased computer use for parents to change their behavior.

Double Standards

And what about the families that don't own a personal computer? Amidst all the hype about the Web and the flashy television commercials touting the wonders of the latest Microsoft software, it's easy to lose sight of the fact that millions of U.S. homes have yet to join the computer revolution. How do these children acquire the skills and confidence they need?

The truth is, many don't. At home and at school, many of these children are shut out of the opportunity to learn and use computers, further widening the gap between those who have access and those who don't.

Some of these children—usually the boys—manage to figure out a way to gain access. They hang out at the computer lab before and after school; they hook up with a friend who has a computer; they find a community center that offers computer classes. They seek out each and every opportunity to get their hands on a keyboard.

Girls typically don't pursue these opportunities, however, and very few people notice—let alone ask why.

Some parents assume (at times correctly) that their daughters simply have a broader range of interests than their sons. Some even go so far as to view their daughter's disinterest in computers as a positive thing—at least when compared to their son's obsession. But that attitude ignores the complicated mix of pressures that help determine whether girls will pursue such activities: pressure from peers, and pressure from home.

Many of the girls I met—some as young as third and fourth graders—didn't have the option of joining an after-school activity. When the school bell rang, they headed home, often with a younger brother or sister in tow. They took care of younger siblings, cleaned the house, prepared the dinner. Rarely did their brothers share these duties.

Family responsibilities aren't the only reason girls don't participate in extracurricular computer activities at the same rate as boys. There's another, much more serious concern that keeps girls from participating in equal numbers: personal safety. Gail Breslow and her staff at the Boston Computer Museum's Computer Clubhouse discovered how critical an issue transportation is when they opened their drop-in computer center in 1993. The center is open weekday afternoons for students from ten to eighteen years of age. It's a tremendous resource, filled with cutting-edge computer hardware and professional-quality software for the students to learn and explore. With adult mentors as their guides, students can create sophisticated multimedia presentations, mix music in the clubhouse sound studio, and use state-of-the-art programming tools to control robots, or create their own computer games. But day after day, the majority of the students taking advantage of all these amazing tools are boys.

The Boston Computer Museum is located on the wharf in downtown Boston, and getting there isn't easy. The closest subway station is a brisk five-minute walk away, and in the fall and winter, when it's dark by 4:30 P.M., most parents don't want their daughters taking public transportation or walking the streets of Boston alone. By the time girls are old enough to have a little more freedom of movement, says Breslow, "We've lost them to other responsibilities and other interests."

That's why she and her staff introduced a girls-only day every Monday, even going so far as to provide transportation for the girls to and from the clubhouse. More recently, Ms. Breslow and her staff have opened several satellite clubhouses closer to the communities in which their members live. Without the issue of transportation to contend with, at least one of these neighborhood facilities has achieved a fifty-fifty ratio between boys and girls.

Will It Blow Up If I Push
the Wrong Button?

The differences between how boys and girls use the computer aren't just about how much time they spend in front of the screen. They're also about how that time is spent. As early as kindergarten, teachers observe boys grabbing the mouse and clicking away, oblivious to and unconcerned with whatever havoc they might wreak. They open files, they click on anything that looks interesting, they stumble around and, eventually, they figure things out. It's not a very efficient approach to learning new software, but this approach has an important by-product: it engenders a tremendous amount of confidence. These young boys are fortified with the confidence that comes with knowing you figured something out for yourself.

Girls, on the other hand, are often afraid to explore, worried what might happen if they do something wrong—a fear that many women carry with them into adulthood. So when a group of third- and fourth-grade girls are treated to an afternoon of unstructured computer time, most of them sit in their chairs, hesitant to even touch the mouse. They wait for instructions and guidance. They can't, they won't, just explore. What if it blows up?

Boys aren't born with some innate ability to tinker, or some intrinsic interest in computers. We cultivate that interest. We give it opportunities to grow—sometimes even to the point of looking the other way as boys ignore other aspects of their physical and social development. Girls rarely receive that kind of support. Among tenth graders polled, for example, slightly more than sixty percent of the girls said they had *never* talked to their parents about science and technology issues, compared to approximately forty-five percent of the boys.[6]

It should come as no surprise that these same boys and girls eventually grow up to be men and women with very different views of technology.

Tools or Toys?

A headline in the *Wall Street Journal* read, "The Gender Divide: A Tool for Women, a Toy for Men; Gender Affects How User Sees the Computer."[7] The article—the first in a five-part series—went on to describe the differences in the way men and women view and use the computer. "While women *use* computers, men love them. Just as men are more likely than women to be enraptured by stereo systems, men seem more likely to be captivated by the computing machine itself," the writer observed. To make his point, he cited as an example a wife and husband who, although they share the same profession and many common interests and hobbies, take a very different approach to computing. "I enjoy the challenge of learning the next technology," the husband is quoted as saying. "I've found that although I don't use the computer that much, I have a theoretical base. I know the jargon. Joan could care less. She wants it to work. She wants to type [her stuff] and be done with it."[8]

Although I could relate to the woman's desire to turn on the computer, complete the task at hand, and move on, I chafed at the stereotype nonetheless. No, I don't like to spend my evenings souping up my PC or shopping at the local computer superstore. But neither am I completely uninterested in how my computer works, the ramifications of new technologies, or in making sure I know enough to fix minor problems as they occur.

Like many women and girls, I'm caught somewhere between the role that's been defined for me and the one I'm trying to define for myself. I've worked for nearly ten years with computer publications, yet I almost reflexively correct anyone who describes me as a "techie." I get excited by some of the new gadgetry, but I'd never pick up a computer magazine and start reading it just for fun. I'm no longer tentative when faced with an unfamiliar application, but neither do I spend time exploring new software just for the heck of it. In my own way, I, too, have bought into the concept that computers are tools for women and toys for men.

Why not consider the computer a tool? A personal computer is an expensive piece of equipment. Doesn't it make more sense, isn't it more productive, to view it as a tool for school, for work, for home? Isn't tinkering and playing games just a waste of time, anyway? Sure, it can be. But tinkering may also lead to creative ideas for new types of hardware. Exploring new software applications—or investigating unused features of a package you use every day—can lead to greater productivity and a better understanding of the myriad tools at our disposal. Playing games can also build and hone problem-solving skills, improve spatial awareness, and help players to think logically. Game playing might even lead to a desire to create games for oneself.

In general, women do tend to view computers as tools, not as expensive, hi-tech playthings. Many men, on the other hand, love to tinker with their system and delight in every new hardware and software purchase. But we need to be careful about such characterizations. Using the computer as a tool doesn't preclude exploring its many capabilities. What of the women who *do* enjoy playing games? What about the girls who *do* like to tinker? When we accept the notion that computers are tools for women and toys for men, we limit our daughters' options. We limit how they see themselves—and how others view them.

A Girl Can't Be a Hacker, Can She?

A team of researchers in Ontario, Canada, spent the better part of the 1994–1995 school year working with a class of twenty-nine seventh and eighth graders. Their goal: to identify the different ways students use computers, and to understand how their gender influenced those patterns of use.

After months of observation and interviews, the researchers divided the students into seven classifications, ranging from "hackers," defined as students who "loved using computers, exploring new software, solving hardware problems, playing games, and creating programs and games of their own," to "luddites," students who "emphatically, repeatedly, and unwaveringly claimed that computers [were] stupid and boring and that they 'hated everything to do with computers.'" There were also several categories in between, among these game players, game creators, reluctant tool users, eager tool users, and sporadic users. As might be expected, many students fell into more than one category. That is, an avid game player often enjoyed creating his or her own games, as well. Similarly, a hacker might also be an eager tool user.

Of the twelve girls in the class, three were what researchers described as eager tool users—students who were quite adept at using all the computer tools at their disposal—from writing and printing homework assignments to creating illustrations or sending e-mail. These students used the computer as needed at home and at school. They were confident in their abilities and frequently turned to one another for advice and assistance.

The second group was what the researchers called

reluctant tool users: five of the girls fit into this category. For this group, computer work was something akin to eating their vegetables. They didn't enjoy it, but they knew it was good for them. (They acknowledged, for example, that computer-generated reports looked better and would therefore receive better grades.) These students weren't self-sufficient, though, and frequently turned to an instructor for help. Several girls were identified as game players or game creators—though the games they created were, for the most part, designed as part of a class assignment. (Many of the boys, on the other hand, created their own games just for the fun of it.)

In the end, girls in the classroom were identified as part of every group of users except one: the hackers. Ironically, it wasn't because none of the girls exhibited hacker tendencies. One girl in the class had comparable skills to all the boys classified as hackers, but she lacked one important characteristic: neither she nor her peers thought of her in that way. Unlike the other categories, the hacker designation carried with it a social aspect as well as a technical one. Hackers, as defined by the researchers, were the students everyone else in the class went to for assistance—even the teacher and the researchers. And though the girl was clearly as adept with computers—and as avid a user as many of the male hackers—it never occurred to anyone in the class—not the teachers, not the students, not even the girl herself—that she, too, was an expert. No one asked her for advice. No one asked her to fix a printer that was acting up or to troubleshoot a software problem. No one recognized her talents.[9]

Given the image that most of us have of hackers—a nerdy guy with poor personal hygiene habits and even worse social skills—few parents would lament their daughter not receiving such a dubious distinction. But put aside all those nerdy images and think for a minute about what it means when we are unable to view girls as highly technical people. How can we expect our daughters to even consider exploring computers and related technologies if the only image they have of someone technical is that of a guy—and not a socially acceptable guy, at that?

Our daughters, like our sons, need to be able to envision themselves as savvy, technical people. But our society doesn't provide young girls with examples of women in technical positions—though there are clearly many, many women who fit that description. That's why modeling must start at home—with mom, and with dad.

2

Does Mom Surf the Net?

Mothers and
Other Role Models

It's every parent's dilemma: how to be a good role model for our children, despite our human foibles. We have ideas about how to teach them to be courteous, and to respect others. We know how to impress upon them the importance of hard work and determination. But how do parents who might not be comfortable with technology make sure they don't transfer that same discomfort to their daughters? What can technically savvy moms and dads do to ensure that their daughters grow up equally sure of themselves in this critical area? How can we as parents, teachers, and concerned adults, make sure that we're not—through our actions or our inaction—steering our daughters away from technology? How can we take advantage of the mother–daughter bonds to foster an appreciation and an interest in technology, rather than fear and insecurity?

Sara Jarvis and Anita Kishel, two classroom teachers at Washington-Carver Elementary School in Muncie, Indiana, understand the power of this mother–daughter bond. The teachers started an after-school program with the help of a fellowship from the American Association of University Women (AAUW) that gives girls and their moms hands-on computer experience, and a glimpse of the many possibilities a technical background can afford.

Two afternoons a month, a group of fourth- and fifth-grade girls and their mothers take over a classroom at their elementary school. Working together, the mother–daughter teams explore the Internet and learn how to use a variety of new hardware and software tools. But these afternoon sessions are about more than just honing basic computer skills. They're about opening doors and discovering new options—for both the parent and the child.

For years, Jarvis watched as eager fourth- and fifth-grade girls were transformed into quiet, uncertain middle schoolers. "I've taught school for twenty years and see so many girls who lose their gumption when they get to middle school," she observes. "They show all this potential in elementary school, then in middle school—nothing. . . . They don't have a clue what's out there for them."

Few of the parents at Jarvis' school—where most of the students qualify for the free lunch program—have college degrees. Many work in relatively low-paying service-sector jobs. For most girls, higher education isn't even a blip on the radar screen. Jarvis recalls taking some of her students to visit a local college and watching as their tour guide asked the girls how many planned on attending the college after high school. Not one girl raised her hand. The thought hadn't even occurred to them.

"I don't know how to arm them, except to make them good in nontraditional things," says Jarvis. But it's not enough to just teach the girls new skills, such as how to use video production equipment or how to design multimedia presentations on the computer. To effect real change requires constant reinforcement—both at school and at home. Who better to help with that process, asks Jarvis, than the girls' mothers?

Many of the moms had never used a computer before starting the program, but now, under the teachers' tutelage, they're learning new skills and then teaching them to their daughters. "The moms learn from us and the daughters learn from the moms," explains Jarvis. "It gives them something they can do on their own, together. The girls depend on their moms a lot more than they depend on us."

Over the course of the school year, the girls, with help and advice from their mothers, researched a specific profession on the Internet, and selected a local woman with a career in that field to interview, videotape, and, ultimately, create a multimedia presentation. The final project, a full-length video chronicling the lives of local professional women, then will be presented at a meeting of the local AAUW chapter.

Many of the mothers in the program work full-time jobs in addition to the demands of caring for their homes and their families. So when the teachers were writing up the project proposal they made sure to ask for funds for what they called "substitute moms," women who could step in and help the girls out when their mothers were unable to attend one of the afternoon sessions. Week after week, though, those funds went unused.

"Every week at the end of the session we're astounded at what these women get done. We look at each other and go, 'wow,'" says Jarvis. "These women have arranged their schedules, found babysitters, and when they can't come, they get their own mother or a sister to come. The mothers have always felt really responsible for making sure they get someone in the family to be there."

The mother–daughter program is a success not because the moms were computer gurus or Web masters. It is successful because the moms were willing to learn, and because these moms recognized how crucial their role is in their daughter's technological development. Some moms are so excited, in fact, that they take advantage of every opportunity to use the computer equipment—even on afternoons when the program isn't in session.

Powerful Stuff

Sara Jarvis and Anita Kishel have tapped into something pretty powerful and they know it. They've managed to take what could have been a reason for these girls to consider high-level computer skills out of their reach—their mothers' lack of interest and lack of experience in this area—and turned it into an incredible learning experience for everyone concerned.

Girls frequently cite their mother as the most influential person in their lives. The person they admire most, the person they most want to be like. And yet, when it comes to computers, many women have never had the opportunity to explore, let alone grow comfortable with, the technology. Instead of seeing their mother as a confident, capable computer user, someone who can just as easily look up a home remedy for poison oak on the Internet as patch them up after a fall, many girls see someone who's unsure of herself, who defers to someone else for assistance, someone who's intimidated by the technology, not empowered by it.

"A lot of parents still don't even notice the messages they're sending to their daughters," says Rita Levinson, founder of a computer training firm in Hillsborough, California, called Screen Play. Levinson, whose background is in computer science and mathematics, is a firm believer in the power of role models to influence a girl's behavior and attitudes. She was one of the organizers of the first Expanding Your Horizons conference, a daylong event designed to introduce preteen and teenage girls to women involved in a variety of math, science, and technology-related careers. "A lot of women don't realize that they're passing on negative images to their daughters," says Levinson. "Every time they say, 'I don't understand computers' or 'Go ask your dad,' they're perpetuating the stereotype that computers are a guy thing."

Girls can certainly learn computer mechanics—how to install a software program, how to format a floppy disk, or how to make their way around the Internet— from just about anyone. There's nothing to say that a woman is better equipped to teach a girl those skills than a man. But it's one thing to have a grasp on the mechanics and quite another to feel as though the technology has a place in your life. For that, girls need to be surrounded by technically savvy, confident women.

Like Mother, Like Daughter

Caroline Lambert knows what an incredible difference it can make to have a mother who enjoys science and technology. Ms. Lambert is a computer scientist with a large company in the San Francisco Bay area. Her mother was a physicist—a field with even fewer women than computer science—and she instilled her love for science in her daughter. "I think it would have made a big difference if my mother hadn't been a physicist," says Ms. Lambert, noting that because of her mom's scientific background, she never had any inhibitions about science and never doubted that the field was wide open to her. "We need more [women] as role models. . . . We need fathers who stay at home and mothers who aren't intimidated by technology," she adds.

But it isn't just girls who want to pursue careers in math or science who need a strong, technically savvy mother as a role model. Every girl needs one. Just as every girl needs to know that it's okay to be female and enjoy sports, or to be female and fix cars, every girl needs to know that whether she aspires to be a fashion designer or a Web page designer, computer skills will be vital to her success. When a girl sees her mother throw up her hands in frustration because she can't figure out how to get the computer to work, she's learning a lesson that's best unlearned. She is learning that somehow women and technology don't go together.

Cindy Cone, a fifth grade teacher at Elmwood Place Elementary School near Cincinnati, Ohio, was dismayed to find that many girls in her afterschool computer club thought they were "stupid as far as computers go." After observing how so many girls doubted their abilities, Cone began to approach her all-girls, after-school computer program differently. She switched from organizing activities for the girls to giving them time to just explore on their own. She sat back and watched as they'd encounter problems and work together to devise a solution. "When I asked them how they felt about not receiving a lot of help from me they said they thought it was pretty neat that they could figure it out for themselves," recalls Cone.

It's so easy to pass along feelings of inadequacy to our daughters where science and technology are concerned. Although I'm the primary computer user in our house, for years I told my children they'd have to wait for their father to get home if they wanted something taped on the VCR. It wasn't that I was incapable of figuring it out— I just had never gotten around to reading the manual. I knew that, but did my children? Over time I realized they stopped asking me for help with the VCR—they just went straight to dad. It's just one more example of why mothers and fathers alike need to be constantly on the lookout for ways in which they might be passing along harmful stereotypes to their children.

Anna Pittioni knows what it's like to work with girls who hold a very traditional view of women. Like Cindy Cone, she organized a science and computer enrichment program for young women at her middle school in Concord, California. To give everyone a chance to get to know each other, Pittioni held a sleep-over at her house at the beginning of the school year. The girls checked out sites on the Internet, played computer games, got into pillow fights, and had a good time. At one point during the evening, one of the girls inadvertently closed the bathroom door—locking the girls and their host out of the much-used room. Try as they might, they couldn't unlock the door. Immediately, the girls started saying, " 'Call your husband to come fix it,' " recalls Pittioni. "They didn't believe me when I said I could help them."

What does fixing a lock on a bathroom door have to do with computers? In a way, everything. It didn't even occur to Pittioni's weekend guests that a woman could be just as handy with a screwdriver as a man. It also never occurred to many of those girls that women could be just as adept at using a computer as men.

"Many of these girls have very traditional mothers and fathers as role models. They just don't see women doing the kinds of things I'm offering to them," says Pittioni. As a result, she says, many of the girls find the technology intimidating. "They don't seem to take the risks; they're really afraid of breaking things; they're afraid of messing something up." But Pittioni is on a mission to show girls that they can master the technology. Through her example, and through her willingness to learn and explore, she is beginning to tear down some of the barriers that have been erected between her girls and computers.

What Dads Can Do

As much as girls need mothers who are unafraid to explore technology, they need fathers who will support their interests and encourage them every step of the way.

When I was in school, I competed in any and every sport. In the fall I'd play tennis, in the winter basketball was my sport, and in the spring of my sixth-grade year I discovered track. At first, I was lukewarm about the idea of making endless trips around the oval track, but over time I developed a passion for the sport that persists even today, thanks, in large part, to my father's encouragement. Several evenings a week he would take my brother and me to a nearby junior college where, stopwatch and tape measure in hand, he would work with us on our sprints, or show us how to eke out another inch in our broad jumps. Never once in all the years we ran track did my father expect any less of me—or do any less to encourage me—than he did for my brother. Looking back, it was those evenings at the track as much as anything else in my childhood that instilled in me the belief that I could do anything my brother—or any other boy—could do.

For many of the girls and women I interviewed for this book, their fathers played a similar role in introducing them to computers. It was dad who bought Suzy the new computer games to explore, and dad who handed articles about the tremendous growth in computer-related jobs to Katrina L., a high school senior trying to decide what to major in when she entered college.

Lisa Shoberg, a systems administrator with a computer engineering degree from Cal Poly, says she pursued the nontraditional major on the suggestion of her dad. "I wanted a field that involved math and logic, because I had loved both when I was younger. My dad helped me to see the opportunities in the field and to take my strengths and apply them." Thanks in large part to her parents' support and encouragement, Ms. Shoberg says she never felt as if there was anything unusual about being interested in—and good at—math and science.

Denise Gúrer, a computer scientist with SRI International, tells much the same story: "My mom is a nurse practitioner and my dad is a physicist. They both always supported me and impressed upon me that I could pursue whatever I wanted. If I wanted to pursue math, I should go ahead and do it. It wasn't a weird thing at all."

But not every young woman receives that kind of support from her father. I spoke to one teacher, for example, who couldn't figure out why one of her female students was so unsure of herself at the computer. She was good in school and confident about so many other things—sports and academics included. And yet, put her in front of the computer and she would fumble around, unsure of what to do or how to do it. And then, one evening, the teacher met the girl's parents and the situation suddenly became a lot clearer.

"Mom and dad both came to a computer training we were offering," recalls the teacher. Mom sat down at the computer and started using the software, but before she could really even begin to explore, dad grabbed the mouse and said, "You can't do it, just give me the mouse."

Both parents were eager to make sure their daughter developed strong computer skills. Neither would intentionally tell her she wasn't smart enough or technical enough to do so. And yet, that's what their actions were telling her every day.

In far too many households, a pattern of behavior has been established where the man is in charge of all things technical. Dad sets up the new cable box. Dad programs the VCR. Dad buys the computer and tinkers with it when things go wrong. After years of observing this behavior, our sons and daughters eventually come to believe that life's technical difficulties are best left to the men to fix. They learn to view women as either uninterested in—or worse, incapable of—taking care of such things themselves.

Positive Signs

Change doesn't come easily. Images of the techie guy and the technically challenged woman are firmly entrenched in our society. Many of us grew up with those images and we have a difficult time shedding them ourselves, let alone offering alternatives for our sons and daughters. And yet, new patterns are emerging that are slowly chipping away at old stereotypes and offering our children new role models.

Although men have historically been more frequent users of home computers than women, that trend is changing. Women represent a rapidly increasing percentage of all Internet users, a percentage that is growing exponentially as more services and Web pages are developed specifically for women. Women own 3.5 million home-based businesses in the United States; they rely heavily on computers, e-mail, fax machines, and cellular phones to keep those businesses running smoothly. [10]

As young girls see their mothers sending e-mail to customers, creating sophisticated multimedia presentations for their next sales call, and faxing contracts to their latest clients, they begin to adopt a new view of women and technology. That same shift occurs each time a girl sees her mother chatting on the Internet or investigating a new CD-ROM. Both types of activities are important if a girl is to get a well-rounded view of the many uses for technology in her life.

Cathaleen Hampton knows the value of modeling certain types of behavior for children. As a third-grade teacher, her actions and attitudes are scrutinized every day by the twenty boys and girls in her class. "My students definitely see that I enjoy computers," says Hampton, laughing. "I model that in the classroom every day. I'm always saying to them, 'Wow, look what I found,' and getting excited about the neat things you can do and great information you can find."

Hampton believes it's especially important to show girls more than just the utility of computers if we truly want them to feel at home in front of a monitor. "These girls are all so production oriented. They want to sit down at the computer and make something. They do need to use it as a tool, but they need to have fun, too." That's why she makes a point of sitting down with her own daughter and playing games. "If it can be a toy for her dad, why can't it be a toy for her, too?"

Starting From Scratch

We don't have to be computer experts to be good role models for our daughters. There's no reason, in fact, why mothers and fathers who aren't computer savvy can't learn right along with their children—even learn *from* their children. It's not how much we know that counts, it's how willing we are to learn. Summoning up and displaying our own curiosity can be inspirational. Even if we've never logged on to the Internet, or have never installed a new software program, we can teach our daughters valuable lessons by being unafraid to explore, and by encouraging them to explore right along with us.

Programs like the one started by Sara Jarvis and Anita Kishel are a great way for mothers and daughters to learn about computers together. Although such activities are rare at most schools, there are other avenues to explore: the Girl Scouts, for example, is redoing its badges and other "recognitions" for computer-related projects, and is encouraging troop leaders and mothers of participating girls to join in the activities. Local chapters of the AAUW, for their part, also offer day-long technology events for mothers and daughters.

Exploring computers with your daughter doesn't have to be part of an organized activity. There's no reason why mothers and daughters can't sit down together one evening a week and investigate a new Web site, explore a chat room, or play a new CD-ROM game.

Computers are a powerful and an *empowering* technology. What could be more fitting than mother and daughter discovering that power—and claiming it as their own—together.

: 3 :

<u>Wanted:</u>
<u>A Game for Me</u>

When it comes to computers, ten-year-old Rachel W. has it made. Sort of. She has her own Web page and enjoys playing with computers almost as much as she likes sports and hanging out with her friends. She even has her own Macintosh, so she doesn't have to fight her brother to get a turn at the mouse. There's just one problem: "A lot of the games seem like they're designed for boys," says Rachel. Sure, there's Monopoly, which she's a whiz at, or The Print Shop, for making cards and invitations. Rachel's even used her brother's computer to try her hand at Castle Wolfenstein, a 3-D action game.

But board games—even electronic ones—get old after a while, and there're only so many cards and letters you can make. As for Wolfenstein, it's not that Rachel *can't* play it—she can take out an enemy with the best of them. It's just that she doesn't want to. What Rachel really wants, what she *longs* for, is a game designed for her—not her older brother.

"There are only men in a lot of the games—and there's no bright colors. It's all droopy," says Rachel, her brilliant yellow turtleneck a sharp contrast to the dark, even sinister colors that dominate the landscape in many popular fighting or action games. Not content to just "make do" with what software companies are cranking out, Rachel thought up her own game. "Want to hear about my idea?" she asks eagerly, then without waiting for an answer she plunges into a play-by-play description: "You're in a jungle, and you're looking for animals that will give you clues about where to find a backpack full of treasure. There are ten animals, but only five have clues, and if you ask the wrong five, all the animals that do have the clues and could help you run away . . ."

Rachel goes on for several minutes describing the details of her game and devising her strategy for winning. The more engrossed she gets, the more excited she becomes—about the challenge, the adventure, and the fun.

Alexa R., also ten years old, stays away from all the gory games. "My parents won't let them in the house," she explains in the tone that lets you know there's no arguing with mom and dad. But it's more than a matter of following the rules. "They just don't interest me," she says with a bored look on her face. "They're dumb."

Rachel and Alexa are at a tough age. When they were younger, educational titles captivated their attention, all the while helping to build important math, reading, and critical thinking skills. As they near adolescence, though, the choices are far fewer and much less compelling. Zany characters and lively music aren't enough anymore. Just as with clothes and movies, they've stopped identifying with "kids'" computer games and have begun casting about for games that are a little cooler, a little less juvenile, a little more grown-up. But when they head to the store to check out the selection, they're often left pushing around an empty shopping cart.

Between *Sesame Street* and Schwarzeneggar

It's eight o'clock on a Monday evening and there isn't a female in sight at the San Francisco-area computer superstore. The salespeople are all men this evening and so are the customers, several of whom are hanging out in the gaming section, checking out the latest CD-ROM titles. Taking up two full rows are the animated 3-D action games, with names such as Hell Bender or Pray for Death. The boxes feature Arnold Schwarzeneggar–types armed to the teeth, or wicked-looking women dressed in short, tight clothes.

Month after month, these are the games that top the best-seller list. Although their developers say they're designed for the eighteen- to thirty-year-old market, boys as young as nine and ten live to play them. They are the carrot that motivates boys to finish their homework or clean up their rooms. They are the subject of endless postings on electronic bulletin boards, where gamers share strategies, compare scores, and brag about their accomplishments. What's their appeal? They're fast-paced, action-packed, and loaded with enough weaponry to blow away a small country.

The blockbuster hit of 1996 was Duke Nukem 3D. Like Doom, or Wolfenstein before it, the object of the game is to kill or be killed. Among its "butt kickin'" features: twenty-seven levels and ten weapons. The description on the box says it all: "Clear crowds with the pump action Assault Shotgun, blast through enemy walls with the Rocket Propelled Grenade, splat enemies under foot after blasting them with the Shrinker . . ."

What does Duke Nukem or the countless other games that feature explicit violence and degrading images of women say to our daughters? What do girls think when they see their male classmates, their brothers, perhaps even their fathers, obsessed with advancing to the next level, and the next, and the next, and the next? Many of the girls I spoke with just shrugged off the titles as stupid and meaningless. But they're also dangerous, for they send a message to our children that devalues women—both on and off the screen.

Less offensive (though certainly not lacking in testosterone quotient) are the sports titles—box after box of games for every type of sports enthusiast: NHL '97, Full

Court Press, NBA Live, Monday Night Football, John Madden Football, Total Control Football, Indy Car Racing, and Nascar Racing, to name just a few. Although the selection isn't as plentiful as the action games (sports titles only fill *one* row in the games section), there are still plenty of titles for the armchair athlete to choose from. And for the would-be soldier, there're close to two dozen military CD-ROM titles—games with names like Nato Fighters, Allied General, Commanche 2, and Command and Conquer.

Those three basic genres fill close to ninety percent of the shelf space devoted to noneducational games. What little space is left is occupied by a hodgepodge of titles, from chess to trivia to an assortment of action/adventure games. One of the most popular titles in the latter category was Myst, a CD-ROM game that managed to captivate the attention of women and girls, as well as boys and men. The "Sim" titles from Maxis have also been popular with both genders. So have games like Carmen Sandiego and Oregon Trail, two long-time hits that girls consistently rate among their favorite titles. Although these games look and feel quite different from one another, they share many important characteristics that researchers have identified as appealing to many girls: they're open-ended; there's no clock ticking away in the background; they can be played for several minutes, or several hours—depending on the player's time and inclination.

Of course girls aren't going to buy only from this latter assortment. Some girls and women enjoy action games, or are fascinated by military history and weaponry. Even more love professional sports. But these games make no effort to appeal to the specific interests of girls and women, or to address these subjects from a female perspective. They're about guys: guys fighting, guys tackling, guys shooting hoops, guys flying jets. When a female does appear, she's typically a supporting character—there to be rescued by the guy, or, of course, to entertain him.

What happens when girls look around and see so few games designed with their interests in mind? When they've already played Wheel of Fortune or Jeopardy! a hundred times and are searching for something new that's challenging and fun? When they see boys their age obsessed with computer games, but can't find any for themselves? Some girls, such as Rachel, discover online entertainment and leave games behind without a second thought. Others explore computer-based creativity tools, such as card-making programs or desktop publishing or photo editing software. But it's at this preadolescent age that many girls' computer use starts to decline. They look around and see nothing that's fun, nothing that can compete with all their off-computer activities. They continue to use the computer as a tool for school work or other types of production, but they stop looking at it as a toy, as a source of fun and entertainment.

"The first thing that influences play is the type of

software that's widely available," says Dr. Maria Klawe, vice president, student and academic services at the University of British Columbia in Vancouver and founder of the E-GEMS project, which studies the role of electronic games in math and science education. Put simply, the more computer games there are for boys, the more boys will play computer games.

That fascination with computer play doesn't stop when the game is over. Often, their devotion to games encourages boys to go further—to explore other aspects of computing. Some try their hand at programming so they can create their own games. Others tinker with the hardware, trying to figure out ways to make the games faster, more fun, more challenging. Those digressions don't occur to most girls. "Most avid gamers don't go on to become software engineers," explains one software executive, "but most software engineers have been avid gamers."

Certainly playing computer games isn't at the top of any parent's wish list for their daughters. Given the choice, most would rather have their daughter outside playing soccer or jumping rope than sitting indoors glued to a computer screen. But there's a facility, an ease that comes with computer use—often acquired through gaming—that children carry with them long after their fascination with computer games has ended. It's something that Dr. Gregory Andrews, a professor of computer science at the University of Arizona, says separates the men from the women in the first-year computer science program. "Boys playing games don't have any fear of the technology," says Dr. Andrews. That ease, that confidence, gives them a leg up on classmates who aren't as comfortable around the computer. "There's so much to learn. Students need to know how to log in, how to get an account . . . anything they've done that makes them comfortable is helpful."

Cindy N. is one of those rarities: a female gamer. At eighteen, she's grown up playing just about every kind of gaming system available—from Atari to Sega to Nintendo, to PC-based games. "When I sit down at the computer I feel like a race car driver behind the wheel," says Cindy, confident that she can do just about anything computer-related she sets her mind to.

Of course, too much game time is just as bad—if not worse—than none at all. Ali Nazar has met many budding young software engineers—adolescent boys who'd rather be sitting in front of a computer screen than doing most anything else. He's the former computer director for a coed summer camp where kids learn rock climbing, kayaking, mountain biking, and how to build their own Web page. Every session, says Nazar, some parents actually have to use the promise of computer time to lure their sons to camp. But what mom and dad *really* want is for their son to get outside, meet some friends, and get a little exercise.

"These are the kids we have to kick out of the [com-

puter] lab to take a hike," says Nazar. Kids who are uncomfortable at the weekly dances or karaoke contests
and are overweight from lack of exercise. These are kids
who can create a software program that would make Bill
Gates proud, but who at the age of ten still haven't
learned how to ride a bike. Nazar recalls one boy who
would run down to the computer lab after lunch and
press his face against the glass partition, waiting impa-
tiently for one of the counselors to open up the room so
he could go back to his computer: his friend.

As much as we want our daughters to become capable, confident computer users, the boys Nazar affectionately refers to as "computer geeks" aren't exactly going
to win any prizes as most well-rounded preteens. Few
parents would want their daughters—or their sons, for
that matter—to become so engrossed in computers that
taking a nature hike or bike riding becomes a chore,
rather than an adventure. We can't use those extreme
examples, however, as an excuse for accepting the status
quo. We need to find ways to encourage girls to use
computers while at the same time achieving some sort of
balance in their lives. We need to find a middle ground.

His and Hers

Some companies are attempting to strike a balance by
creating CD-ROM titles they believe will appeal to
young men and young women alike. Microsoft is taking

that route. Its first title for teens is called, Beyond the Limit: Ultimate Climb, a rock-climbing adventure in which players can choose either boys or girls as their central characters. Theatrix Interactive, a small CD-ROM developer, has also decided to go with titles they hope will appeal to both sexes. "I don't want to make a girls-only product," says Theatrix creative director and founder Joyce Hakansson. "It's too stereotypical. Girls are part of the human family. We need to find our way in it." Hakansson has created Hollywood and Hollywood High, two CD-ROM titles in which players write, direct, and perform their own animated shows. Hakansson fully expects the titles will appeal more to girls than they will to boys, but she's consciously kept the packaging and the literature neutral, so as not to scare off male buyers.

Hakansson isn't alone in her approach—though other developers are producing "gender neutral" games for practical, as opposed to philosophical, purposes. Even as developers try to incorporate more features into games they think girls will like, they're careful not to make the products look like they're for girls.

Still others wonder if a girls' market is really viable, given the dynamics of the computer entertainment industry today. Judith Lange is sympathetic to the needs of adolescent girls. She has a daughter of her own and started CAPS Productions, a small software production firm in San Francisco, California, intending to "go after" the girls' market. She even had an option to develop a

series of sports titles featuring famous women athletes—
something like the female version of John Madden Football or Jack Nicklaus Golf. But when it came time to run the numbers, Lange says she just couldn't make it work. "What I learned from young female athletes was that if they enjoy soccer, they want to go *play* it. They don't even *think* of using a computer for that purpose," says Lange. The bottom line: as much as she would like to develop games for girls, Lange is unconvinced that they would buy them. "Areas that are neutral are a little safer," she adds.

It's easy to find numbers to support those concerns: Sixty-three percent of all CD-ROM game buyers are male, according to the Software Publishers Association's 1996 Consumer Survey. And they aren't just buying CD-ROM titles for the kids. They're also playing the games. In the same survey, 66% of all the respondents said the primary user of game and entertainment CD-ROM titles was also male.[11] Software company executives look at those numbers, throw up their hands, and say why bother? Girls don't buy computer games. Girls don't play computer games. Why should we waste our time and money creating something they'll never use?

But these statistics ignore one crucial factor: There aren't enough games out there that interest girls to really know whether girls would spend their money on them.

Not every company is stymied by these statistics, though. A handful of companies—most led by women—

are developing games exclusively for and about girls. No compromises. No apologies.

Girls Just Want to Have Fun

None of these new products has met with more controversy than McKenzie & Co., a live-action adventure set at Madison High, an upper-middle-class school in Anytown, USA. The producer, Her Interactive, was the first company to publicly declare its commitment to developing software for girls, and it chose as its target market the toughest crowd of all: girls between the ages of ten and fifteen. The executives at Her Interactive did their homework. They surveyed 2000 girls and asked them what they wanted most from a computer game. The most common responses: "Cute guys, dating, shopping, telephone conversations, a prom, and music." And that's exactly what they got in McKenzie & Co. The game revolves around getting a guy to ask you to the prom. Along the way you go shopping, hang out with your friends, do some homework, and work at an after-school job so you have enough money to buy a dress for the Big Night.

Considering the game's focus on boys and clothes and dating, it's no surprise that McKenzie & Co. met with a fair amount of backlash. Given all we know about the fragile self-esteem of preteen and teenage girls, and their obsession with fitting in and looking pretty, a game about catching a boy isn't exactly what most of us would pick for our daughters. Too often, the notion of software for girls gets translated into girly software—software that perpetuates all the stereotypes our daughters could just as well do without. True, the girls in McKenzie & Co. struggle with having to balance work and play, and they wrestle with the true meaning of friendship. But these potentially redeeming qualities are overshadowed by the focus on boys as the ultimate prize for doing well in school and working hard—even if, as one company executive says, "it's what girls want."

Some of them, at least.

When Crystal W.'s family bought their new computer, McKenzie & Co. was the first game she played. She'd first read about the game in *Sassy* magazine and had been eagerly awaiting the day when she could try it out for herself. She even set her alarm for 5:45 A.M.—an hour earlier than usual—so she could beat her brother to the computer and play for an hour or so before getting ready for school. "I'd get really absorbed," says Crystal. "I even found myself talking like the girls in the game when I got to school, you know?" she adds, laughing as she thinks about it.

The problem with McKenzie, says Crystal, wasn't the subject matter—it was that there wasn't *enough* of it. Once you go through the game and have tried to get each of the four boys to ask you out, there's not much to do. "I even tried doing all the things you wouldn't do— like doing everything I could to have him *not* ask me to the prom," says Crystal. "And when he did ask me, I said no." That approach met with disappointing results, though. "All it said was, 'Game Over. Would you like to meet another guy?'"

McKenzie & Co. was one of the first of the new genre of girls' software, but it was by no means the biggest hit. That designation goes to one of the most infamous role models for girls of all time: Barbie. Mattel Media burst onto the interactive game scene in late 1996 with three Barbie CD-ROM titles and proceeded to rack up sales the minute the powder-pink boxes hit the shelves. One of the products, Barbie Fashion Designer, which enables users to design their own Barbie clothes, was one of the best-sellers in the 1996 holiday season, outselling many of the traditional games—games that boys like to play.

Like McKenzie, Barbie represents a dilemma for many parents who want their daughters to enjoy using the computer, but who object to the ideal Barbie's hourglass shape and carefully sculpted feet represent. I know that I headed to my appointment to see a demonstration of Barbie Fashion Designer more than slightly irritated at the notion of seeing Barbie on the computer screen. And yet, I left that meeting with mixed feelings. The product was well done. It was cool. It was different. It was, well, fun.

We Want Barbie!

It's six o'clock on a cold December evening and a group of elementary-age girls have just arrived at the Computer Clubhouse at the Patriot's Trail Girl Scout office in Boston's Back Bay. The girls, all residents of a local housing project, are one of several area groups—some Girl Scout troops, some not—that use the new center every week.

The girls are eager to get started, but they aren't interested in creating holiday cards, the activity that's been planned for them tonight. "We want to play Barbie," says one girl. "I never got to do Barbie," chimes in another. "I want to do Barbie," shouts a third, raising her arms high up into the air to catch the attention of the clubhouse manager, Juliana Yu. Juliana shoots me a look that says, "I told you this would happen."

Before the girls had arrived that evening, Juliana and I had sat down and talked about the clubhouse, and about the night two weeks earlier when the same group of girls discovered the famed Barbie software. Juliana had never intended to show the girls the package, but one of the girls spotted it on a shelf and—much to her dismay—that's all any of them have asked about ever since. "I have to hide the software," she said ruefully. "I'm afraid if we show it to another group of girls we're going to turn into the Barbie Doll Clubhouse."

Juliana shares a debate she's been having with herself over the product. "On the one hand, it's good, because you can very easily get them interested, get them in front of the computer." Some of the girls, she adds, came out of their shell after playing with the Barbie software. "After the Barbie incident, when I told them I had some really cool software, they would try it. It's like having the Barbie software here built their trust, made them think, 'They have cool things here.' "

"But girls shouldn't be surrounded by Barbie stuff," she adds, still unsure if the end—getting girls excited about computers and willing to try new software—justifies the means.

For me, the answer to that question is made all the more difficult by the absence of a wide selection of software for preteen girls. When you walk down the software aisle and the majority of games for girls this age has Barbie in the title, the negative images become that much more pronounced. In the end, my daughter and I did design an outfit or two using Fashion Designer— and we both had fun doing it. But I've also made sure she understands there's much more to computers than those eye-catching pink boxes that today are all the rage.

Not Your Brother's
Software

Although she's taken center stage, Barbie is not the only CD-ROM game in town. Like Mattel and Her Interactive, a few upstart computer game companies are releasing their versions of games for girls. They're in the business to sell products, but in the process, they hope to get girls excited about computers, give them confidence in their abilities, and let them have some fun.

The execution of that goal has taken many forms, from interactive diaries to games and adventures in which smart, spunky girls take center stage. Some companies are capitalizing on "hit properties," like Sabrina the Teenage Witch or Pleasant Company's American Girl Doll collection, in order to bring girls to the computer. Others, like Purple Moon and Girl Tech, are starting from scratch, developing their own unique cast of characters who they hope will resonate with girls and young women. They're also moving beyond the traditional computer game in an attempt to bridge activities on and off the screen. Girl Tech, for example, is working with local Girl Scout councils to develop computer badges and "recognitions"; the company also plans to develop a line of high-tech toys for girls. Purple Moon, for its part, will introduce dolls, cards, and collectible stones to go along with its games.

All of these choices bode well for the future. Girls now have options that didn't exist even a few years ago. Will these new games captivate the attention of *all* young girls? Probably not. Games for girls aren't *the* answer to the inequities surrounding girls and computers. But they are *part of* the answer. The broader the selection of software, the greater the likelihood that our daughters will find something to excite and challenge them, and to convince them that computers can be as much a source of fun as they are of learning. The next generation of these games also share one more key characteristic: Internet access, so the game playing and adventure can extend well beyond the capabilities of the single CD-ROM. Given girls' fascination with the Web, that could be a match made in heaven.

: 4 :

My Place in Cyberspace

"It's kind of like my little area on the Web. All those big companies have pages and pages and pay people thousands of dollars to make them, but I have made up my own. It's kind of like my house or my child. It's one of the few things in life you have complete control over."

Nico J. is fourteen—an age when many girls don't feel as if they have control over much of anything in their lives. But on the World Wide Web, she and thousands of girls are finding a place where they can express themselves freely and without reservation, where they can meet men, women, boys, and girls, and be judged not by their age or their gender (provided, of course, they don't disclose those critical details), but by their words and their actions. Online, they can become part of a community of friends that offer one another advice and support, praise and camaraderie.

Although much has been said and written about the largely male culture of the Web, the worldwide network of computers is taking on a decidedly feminine quality as girls and women eagerly stake out their own territory. Their signposts have names like Nico's Place and Alana's Home on the Web. You can find everything from professionally created and maintained sites, to home-grown pages designed and crafted by girls themselves. The colors are sometimes soft pastels, sometimes bright primary colors. The pages are decorated with psychedelic flowers and smiley faces reminiscent of the sixties and seventies, along with colorful cartoon characters such as Pooh and Piglet, Simba and Aladdin. And they're all decidedly—sometimes defiantly—pro-girl, carrying slogans such as "Girl Power," "Girls Rule," and "Girls Can Do Anything."

The Making of a Web Girl

Nico began going online when she was nine years old and her parents bought her a new computer and a subscription to Prodigy, a private, commercial online service. "It's funny," she recalls, "all I really knew I could do back then was send e-mail to my penpals and play the online version of Carmen Sandiego. I never won a game, but I just had to play every day anyway." Nico remembers vividly the day she graduated to live chats, the next course in her online education. It was New Year's Eve 1994 and she was at a party at a friend's house. When the clock struck midnight, one of the adults suggested the kids log on to an America Online chat room and wish the other kids "Happy New Year." "I had no idea what a chat room was," says Nico, but she quickly figured it out. "I spent the next two hours in front of the screen. I couldn't believe I was talking to them and they were responding instantly," says Nico excitedly as she remembers that first rush all over again. "I thought, 'Wow. *This* is cool.'"

Nico got her own America Online account and quickly became devoted to life online. The girl who couldn't get excited about programming classes in school, who said she wasn't really into computers and practically "gave them up" when she was nine, was suddenly fired up about this great new technology. She frequented the chat rooms in the Kids Only section of the service, then gradually began exploring other areas, including the Star Trek forum, where she met many of the people that remain her closest online friends. When AOL established its Internet hookup in 1995, Nico was off and running— no longer the computer ingenue who thought going online meant sending e-mail to penpals.

Now, Nico has her own Web page. She's even created one for her mother's band. She pored over detailed coding specifications to figure out how to design and create her own page. She'd been impressed by a friend's homepage and wanted people to feel that same awe and respect when they saw hers. "I did it for the challenge," explains Nico. "I wanted to see if I could teach myself to do it. I told myself, 'I'm going to have a page and everyone is going to think it's cool,' so I sat at my computer and stared and stared at the screen. Finally, it came to me. I worked it all out in my head and it all made sense."

The result of that brainstorm is a place with all the attitude and life you would expect from a fourteen-year-old. The opening screen features a picture of Nico and one of her many pets, a black cat named Toby. In big, bold letters she asks the question, "What's a Nico?" Then promptly sets to answering it.

> "Born December 19, 1982 as a girl, which I still happen to be . . . I've been a veggie for 3½ years and my house has animals moving in every corner. I like to sing, write, read, draw, paint, play soccer n' basketball and surf!!! (surf the web, that is)."

Nico's path from keypal (the term used to describe online penpals) to Webgirl is one that is being traveled by more and more girls throughout the United States and the world. From girls as young as seven—often working with the help of a parent or older friend—to young women starting college, these Webgirls are creating their own space, sharing with the world who they are and what they care about. They're pioneers, blazing a trail in uncharted territory. They go online looking for fun, but the longer they stay, the more they learn—about themselves, the world around them, and the technology that is changing their lives.

There's No Place Like Home

"Purple Haze," by Jimi Hendrix, begins playing when you enter Alana's Home on the Web. The guitar instrumental seems an odd accompaniment to the Pooh silhouettes that fill the background of Alana J.'s homepage, but it's only one of many examples of the complicated mix of innocence and edginess that make up many of today's teenage girls. Consider Alana's "stats," as she describes them on her opening page:

NAME: *Alana (duh)* ← *Click for a picture of me*
AGE: *13*
HAIR COLOR: *Blonde*
EYE COLOR: *Blue-Green*
HEIGHT: *About 5'2"*
WEIGHT: *84 pounds*
INTERESTS: *Writing, shopping, movies, watching TV, Sanrio, Pooh*
FAVE MOVIES: *Twister, Clueless, Winnie-the-Pooh*

FAVE TV SHOWS: *Drew Carey Show, Homicide,*
Murder One, Seinfeld

HATES: *Mushrooms, Wranglers (jeans), country*
music, grasshoppers

STYLE: *Union Bay jeans, Levi's, vintage, polyester*
*shirts, Vans, dELiA*s*

FAVE COLOR: *Purple*

FAVE SANRIO CHARACTERS: *Picke Bicke &*
Purin

From that terse, but nonetheless informative description, Alana goes on to share some of her poetry, highlight her friends' homepages, and point visitors to other cool spots on the Web: Pooh and Tigger stuff, Gund, and the Sanrio and Disney sites, to name a few. Like Nico's page, Alana's Home on the Web is all about Alana: what she wants to say, places she likes to go, and things she likes to do. "What's cool about homepages is that they're about what *you* like," says Alana. "You can make them covered with Pooh if you want, or have lots of poetry, or whatever."

So, while many of the homepages created by girls follow the same basic format (name, age, hobbies, and so on), there's plenty of room for creative interpretation. Each girl has adapted her page to fit her own personal style. Alana pushes Pooh; Ellen H. starts her page off with a quote from Lewis Carroll; and Kerri S. has no characters at all—just a spinning globe and her own story, from birth to age eleven.

It would be easy for a casual visitor to label these sites as "cute," or to write them off as nothing more than teenage girls' online journals. But they are so much more than that. Although friends, family, pets, and hobbies are the first things most girls highlight on their pages, many use the space to tackle difficult, often controversial issues, as well. Fourteen-year-old Ellen takes time out from talking about her horse to discuss her "righteous causes," namely free speech, both at her Catholic high school and on the Internet. Her page sports a blue ribbon from the Free Speech Online Blue Ribbon Campaign, and she writes, "The Internet is a breeding place for ideas, *good* and *bad*, and it should stay that way. Viva la Free Speech!" Cheryl advocates a movement called "The Line Around the World," an Internet-based effort "to get people all around this beautiful planet of ours to be nice to each other." Through her own poetry, twelve-year-old Marsha mourns the death of young children in the Oklahoma City bombing, then points visitors to another spot on the Web for information on how to assist victims of the disaster and their families.

On their homepages, in chat rooms, on message boards, and in electronic newsletters, girls are discovering a new communications vehicle—one that connects them to the world and to each other. They're talking about everything from embarrassing moments to troubles with mom and dad, from abortion to politics. They're sharing tips on how to add new features to their pages, handing out awards to one another for cool designs, and forming friendships as powerful as anything in the "real" world.

The Virtual Community

Nowhere is the sense of community more powerful than in the dozens of clubs girls have formed online. They have names such as Girls Internationally Writing Letters (GIRL, for short), Just for You, GirlWorld, Girls Gathering Club, Cyber Sisters, and Girls Around the World. Many girls belong to several clubs at once and use their homepages to recruit new members.

Some clubs last only a few weeks; others have survived more than a year and boast hundreds of girls as members. Each club has its own Web page, complete with rules for participation, answers to frequently asked questions (FAQs), and links to all its members' sites. Many clubs publish weekly newsletters or invite girls to submit stories, poetry, or their "most embarrassing moment" for publication online. Some clubs send out lists of weekly activities for their members, from completing the sentence, "I love you more than . . ." to coming up with entries for a new advice column. Although some clubs are coed, many are just for young women. The reason? "To show boys that girls can do everything they can do," explained one club president.

Twelve-year-old Alana belongs to "a bunch" of clubs: the Sanrio Club, Girls Only, GRIN, Friends Forever, and Young People World-Wide Sending E-mail. Why join so many? "It's a great way to get penpals and make friends on the Net. And it's cool," she explains. She even had her own club for a while called "Just For You," until she got too busy to handle all the responsibilities associated with it.

Nico hasn't joined any clubs, but she's become part of two online communities all the same: She's the co-president of *The Voice*, a weekly online newsletter that's distributed to more than 2000 teenage members around the world, and she's become active in Star Trek role-playing games—or RPGs, as they're known—on America Online. Twice a week for about two hours she takes on the role of Lieutenant Commander Nico J, and acts out original scripts online with other Trekkies like herself. She's good at it, too. So good, in fact, that she was named the youngest host in the history of the forum.

Just as Nico's addiction to Star Trek led her to the role-playing games, other girls gravitate to forums about their favorite hobby or subjects that appeal to them—from pets to horses to American Girl dolls. They share stories, offer one another advice, and almost always wind up finding a new keypal with whom to correspond. They're also visiting sites designed just for them—places such as the Web pages prepared by Girl Tech, Girl Games, or Purple Moon, all of which include stories, games, and online conversations with other girls their age.

Online clubs, discussion groups, and sites for girls provide more than just a place to talk about the latest teen idol or compare notes on one another's parents. Many of the online sites go out of their way to promote girls and women in technology-related fields. They encourage girls in their pursuit of nontraditional interests and professions, and give them a venue for meeting other girls with like interests.

The support and encouragement girls receive from one another is critical, since many girls don't have friends and schoolmates who share their interest and excitement in computers. If it weren't for virtual communities, these girls might very well wind up saying forget it to computers, rather than running the constant risk of being labeled a geek or weirdo by their peers at school. These relationships also play an important role for young girls just beginning to discover the Web. The links girls provide to favorite pages, and the tips and tricks they offer for surfing the Web, can be like having your very own tour guide to show you all the cool spots and introduce you to new friends.

Who Do I Want to Be Today?

To be an adolescent girl is to be constantly judged by your peers. It's no surprise, then, that girls repeatedly cite the ability to be whoever they want to be as one of the key attractions of going online. "I feel more open online," says Darlene G. "I can become a whole new person. I can behave totally differently than I do with my regular friends. Then the next day I can be someone else."

In *Girls in the Middle*, the AAUW investigates the many different ways girls negotiate school. They try on different roles throughout their middle-school career, sometimes being assertive, other times holding back. The same happens online. Through their electronic communications, girls are able to try on new personas, be bolder than perhaps they feel they can be in person—and then get used to their new self, or discard it for something— or someone—else.

Online, girls aren't judged solely by their clothes, their looks, or their age. They're judged by their ideas and their ability to communicate them. Many girls revel in the newfound freedom to express themselves and have conversations with adults who actually *listen* to their thoughts, to just be *themselves*. "I get to meet a lot of adults online," says Suzy. "They accept what I'm saying much more than if I were talking to them face-to-face," she adds, noting, "and they're always surprised when they find out my age."

Suzy remembers the time she was helping out in the technical support area of eWorld, an online service run by Apple Computer, and an Apple employee sent her e-mail asking if she'd like a job. "When I told him my age [she was thirteen at the time] he was completely shocked," recalls Suzy. He was also pretty impressed. "He tried to work out a way for me to volunteer at Apple, but I was too young, so even that didn't work out."

But as much as they like the compliments when

adults find out how old they *really* are, many girls refrain from disclosing their age or their gender online. One reason is to avoid online harassment, but the other is to avoid the all-too-common bias they're confronted with when people know they are teenage girls. "A lot of times I don't say how old I am," says Nico. "The minute you say you're a girl and thirteen, they think you're stupid and that you're not going to understand things."

Despite the biases, Nico says she has formed friendships online that she knows would never happen in the "real" world. She's become close friends with a forty-year-old woman and a thirty-two-year-old man. Both are married, with lives very different from her own, but both are kindred spirits of a sort, says Nico. Many of her adult online friends are also very protective of her comings and goings. "They ask me who I'm talking to and how old they are. It's like they're my online parents," she groans.

Innocence Lost

As much as Nico might chafe at the overprotective attitude of some of her adult friends, many parents would be relieved to know that someone was watching out for their daughter online. Concerns about online safety are not unfounded. At some point, just about every girl who's active online will be confronted with obscene language, suggestive messages, or outright harassment. Although these offenses rarely extend beyond the confines of cyberspace, every report about a child molester abducting someone he or she met online, or a headline about pornography on the Internet, sends a new group of parents running to shut off the modem and disconnect their daughter from cyberspace.

As a mother, I cringe each time I hear a story about some liaison that's been formed or an abduction that has occurred between an adult and a child online, and yet I also know that such instances are rare and that common sense and an open line of communication between parent and child go a long way toward ensuring safe surfing. Parents with younger children can explore the Web with their daughters, using any one of a number of search engines to identify sites of interest. Older girls aren't going to want their mom or dad sitting by their side while they're chatting or sending e-mail, but parents must take care to go over the ground rules for online activity, much as you would discuss safety concerns the first time your daughter goes to the mall or the library by herself. The precautions are fairly straightforward: children should not disclose their full name (first name is typically okay); neither should they disclose their phone number or address to anyone online. Many children use screen names that make it difficult to tell their gender, let alone any more personal information.

Marian S. is all too aware of the dangers in cyberspace. Her daughter Kerri is an online regular. She's a member of several online clubs, has keypals all over the country, and has a Web page that tells the world all about herself.

Although it was Marian who introduced Kerri to the Web and encouraged her to create her own homepage, she still worries about her daughter's forays into cyber-space—and the no-holds-barred manner in which girls share information with the rest of the world.

"It's great to see the girls' pages," says Marian, "but you just never know who they're sharing all that infor-mation with." Kerri doesn't use the chat facilities very often, says Marian. "I'm reluctant to have her go into those areas. You never know who's there." When Kerri does go in a chat session, she stays alert and checks out the surroundings just like she would when visiting an unfamiliar neighborhood in her city. "I always wait a sec-ond or two before I start talking," says Kerri. "I like to see if there is anyone I know before I start chatting."

Nico, too, is cautious online. "I never put myself in a situation that I can't get out of," she explains, noting that one good thing about being online is that you can always leave when someone makes you feel uncomfortable.

As an extra precaution, parents should always investi-gate new chat areas with their daughters, rather than let-ting them explore these sites on their own. Many of the chat rooms—even those ostensibly set up for children and young adults to talk about hobbies or books or movies—have turned into virtual pick-up scenes. New-comers are often asked to give their "stats," and with many older teens and adults participating in the chats the conversation can quickly take a vulgar turn. One mother of three girls told me she has established a firm rule that bedroom doors are to remain open when her daughters are online. It's a policy worth emulating.

While safety is clearly the biggest concern for parents whose children are exploring cyberspace, there's another issue that children and adults alike need to be aware of before going online. In a groundbreaking report called "Web of Deception," The Center for Media Education in Washington, DC, exposed the many ways in which companies are using online sites to collect personal information about children and market their products to these youngest of consumers.[12]

Offers of free gifts and contests entice children to provide demographic information about themselves. Fun games and puzzles, or a chance to download a new screen saver, keep children coming back to commercial sites. Every minute they spend clicking around on the Rice Krispies or Power Ranger or Bonnie Bell page, their activities are potentially being tracked. Ultimately, companies have the ability to create custom pages for each visitor based on his or her previous use patterns—a subtle and insidious form of direct advertising.

As every parent knows, Saturday morning television consists of little but direct marketing to children. However, the nature of the solicitation is different online than it is on the TV. Unlike Saturday morning commercials, which are clearly identifiable as such, it's become almost impossible to distinguish an advertising site from a content-driven Web page.

How do we protect our children from this type of manipulation, while still giving them the freedom to explore cyberspace? First, we become familiar with the Internet ourselves. We discuss with our children the differences between editorial sites and advertising-driven sites. And, as with issues of safety, we make sure they know not to give out detailed personal information—even if it means they're not eligible for "cool prizes."

Worth the Risk

As much as parents need to understand the dangers, they also need to recognize the tremendous benefits girls gain when they go online. Not only do they gain invaluable computer skills, but their online accomplishments have a positive impact on life off the computer, too. Andrea D.'s mom, Chris, marvels at how confident and self-assured her eleven-year-old daughter has become since she began exploring the Internet and other computer activities. "This is giving her a head start," says Chris. "A lot of girls are afraid of computers. We wanted to make sure that didn't happen with Andrea. That's why we bought her her own computer."

Even chatting, sending e-mail, and posting messages on electronic bulletin boards—activities that might be construed as frivolous by some parents—can prove constructive. As with working on one of the many electronically distributed teen newsletters, these online activities help girls to improve valuable communication skills and to develop and articulate their opinions on many issues.

For many girls, the monitor and keyboard hold little attraction until they go online for the first time. Suddenly, the cold, unsociable machine is transformed into a highly interactive device. That's what happened to Sarah H., a seventeen-year-old high school senior who had used computers for homework assignments throughout high school, but had never had any desire to explore the technology any further. Then she found the Internet. "It was like a whole world opened up to me," says Sarah. She created her own Web page—about horses, her first favorite subject (computers being her second)—then went on to create pages for her teachers, too.

Will every girl who goes online be transformed into a computer whiz, or rush to sign up for a computer science class at school? Of course not. Many girls will stop at e-mail and chatting, or go online only long enough to research a term paper. But it's a start. With each visit, they become more comfortable, more confident computer users. And for those girls that find a home in cyberspace, the results can be truly incredible. The Internet provides them an avenue to explore the technology on their own terms. It serves as an entrée into a much bigger world—a world of computing that might otherwise be closed to them. It's the beginning of a journey that will last a lifetime.

Part 2: Jane@School

: 5 :

Wired Classrooms

On April 19, 1997, hundreds of thousands of volunteers converged on schools throughout the country. Their mission: to connect classrooms, libraries, and school offices to the Internet. Parents and their children, teachers and principals, area business owners and community volunteers spent one long day laying cable, pulling wire, and moving their children one step closer to the much-vaunted Information Superhighway.

The massive wiring effort, part of NetDay 2000, was a vivid illustration of Americans' belief that access to computers is a critical component of our children's education. It's a belief shared by eighty percent of all Americans, who think teaching computer skills is "absolutely essential," according to a 1995 study by Public Agenda.[13] It's shared by school boards, PTAs, and district and school technology committees. It's shared by residents in the Bethel School District, in Oregon and the New Haven School District in California, two communities that passed multimillion-dollar bond measures to ensure that their schools would have the funds necessary to purchase computers, access the Internet, and train teachers in the effective use of technology in the classroom.

Even politicians and their appointees have signed on for the ride. President Clinton identified Internet access for all twelve-year-olds as a cornerstone of the education reform effort he launched at the start of his second term in office. And when Secretary of Education Richard Riley presented his long-range technology plan to Congress in June 1996, he described computers as the "new basic," and the Internet as the "blackboard of the future." As we near the twenty-first century, when an estimated sixty percent of all jobs will require computer or networking skills, few parents or educators would disagree with that assessment. Agreement on the importance of the tools, though, doesn't necessarily translate into equal access and equal opportunities for all of our children. We are a long way from ensuring that all our daughters and our sons share equally in the bounty of technological riches.

Tomorrow's Classrooms Today

Caught up in the computer craze, elementary, middle, and high schools around the country are writing (and rewriting) technology plans, establishing acceptable use policies for students with Internet access, and grappling with the many questions associated with incorporating computers into classroom instruction.

Amidst all the planning and purchasing, parents and educators alike need to constantly ask how our children are benefiting from the influx of computers into schools. Are they learning the basics, such as how to type, and how to use common applications, such as word processors and spreadsheets? Have schools taken the integration of technology one step further and started using computers to increase students' creativity, sharpen their analytical skills, and improve their ability to communicate?

That's what's happening at so-called "technology rich" schools—schools in which the curriculum, perhaps even the school day, has been modified to make the most effective use of computers and related technology. Students at these schools use computers to research and write papers, and to prepare and give presentations; they use them to sort and analyze data, and to communicate with people in the next class or clear around the world. But students' knowledge and expertise often go beyond simply the mechanics of using the hardware and software. Researchers have found that in these technology-rich schools, students often become independent learners and self-starters; they learn to work collaboratively with teachers and with peers; they are more motivated and have a more positive outlook toward their future and the role computers will play in their business and personal lives.

At Taylorsville Elementary School in Taylorsville, Indiana, for example, computers and related technology are used to support self-paced, individualized learning. Students work in teams, based on their abilities in core subject areas—so a student may be in a fifth-grade reading group, a fourth-grade math group, and a sixth-grade science or history group. Students and teachers have access to computers in their classrooms, in the lab, and in the library, all of which are networked together. Naturally, teachers are an integral part of the technology-based reform effort. They've participated in extensive technology training to ensure that they have the comfort and skills necessary to tailor programs to meet the needs of individual students.[14]

The rewards for students who attend these technology-rich schools are many. Lindsey K. is an eighth grader who has benefited from a rich exposure to a variety of computer resources and activities. She's learned how to research science and history projects on the Internet, how to organize and analyze data in a spreadsheet, and how to create sophisticated multimedia presentations to explore topics addressed in social studies and French classes. With each new activity she's gaining a deeper appreciation for the ability of computers to change the way we process and communicate information. "We had an author come visit the school who said computers let you think differently," says Lindsey, stopping for a minute before adding, "They really do."

Lindsey's school hasn't invested as much money as some schools in computers and related technology, but its teachers and administrators have spent a great deal of time developing computer-related projects that will enhance traditional classroom learning. They've also designed new classes that take advantage of these powerful tools, such as multimedia design and animation courses.

Not-So-Equal Access

Although the potential is tremendous, at most schools the reality of computer use falls far short of the ideal. A 1996 RAND study that lauds the achievements of technology-rich schools goes on to note that such examples are rare. The average school "still makes limited use of computers and substantial numbers of schools have very limited access to technology of any kind."[15]

Consider these statistics: only four percent of all U.S. schools have one computer for every five students (that's the ratio deemed adequate to allow regular use by all students). On average, there's one computer for every nine students, but the gap between the haves and the have-nots is huge: in more than half of our schools, the ratio is twenty-five or more students for every computer. In many schools the equipment is outdated, often incapable of running today's software or accessing the Internet.

Smaller schools, secondary schools, and schools in more affluent areas tend to have fewer students sharing computers. Low-income students and students of color have the least access to computer technology, with Hispanic students using computers less often at school than any other ethnic group. They're also using them for less complex tasks, such as playing drill-oriented math and reading games, rather than using the computer to track and analyze data in a spreadsheet, or to organize and prepare a presentation or report.

The disparity in access is compounded by the fact that the same students who rarely use a computer at school are also the least likely to have a computer at home. White Americans are two to three times more likely to own a personal computer than African Americans or Hispanic Americans. Rural poor are the least likely of all groups to own a computer. At home and at school they're deprived of one of the most powerful, versatile educational tools of their time.

The Double Bind

Unequal access has profound implications for all students, but it has a particularly acute effect on girls. When equipment is in short supply—whether it's Bunsen burners, microscopes, or personal computers—the less assertive students are most often the least likely to get their turn. They sit back and let the most aggressive students—most often the boys—grab the tools. So when two, three, or four students need to share a computer for a group project, it's typically the most knowledgeable, the most confident student that has his hand on the mouse, directing the assignment and mastering the tool.

"When there are just a couple of computers per class, everyone might be assigned the same research project, but not everyone is doing it," says Dr. Patricia Campbell, a specialist in gender equity issues who consults regularly with schools throughout the United States. "I guarantee that the kids in charge of the search will be the ones with the most experience." It's the teacher's responsibility, says Dr. Campbell, to structure computer time such that every student has an opportunity to build the requisite skills. "It's not an equity issue," she emphasizes. "It's a good teaching issue."

Any Two, Any Time

During the 1994–1995 and 1995–1996 school years, researchers Rena Upitis and Corina Koch went back to middle school. Working with a class of seventh and eighth graders in a predominantly white, middle-class Ontario, Canada, suburb, they observed the ongoing student dynamics of classroom computer use. As part of the research project, the class had been given four Macintosh computers equipped with a variety of educational software packages. Students were allowed to use the computers on a first-come, first-served basis during math time and during technology time (provided they'd completed all their other work).

The boys in the class loved having access to the computers. Every day they'd sit as close as they could to the workstations and then rush to see who would be lucky enough to nab one of the few available seats. But the girls never joined in the game. In fact, unless they were explicitly asked by the teacher if they needed to use one of the computers to finish an assignment—i.e., unless they were given permission to do so—the girls didn't use the computers at all. Every day during computer time, the boys played games or worked online on projects, but the girls chose other activities. They put finishing touches on assignments, worked on group projects, helped their classmates with their work—they did everything but work with the computers.

Concerned about the inequitable use patterns that had developed during the first year of the project, Upitis and her colleagues worked with the teacher to devise ways to make sure girls and boys shared equally in computer time. Their solution: to designate two computers for the boys and two for the girls. Since girls were hesitant to compete with boys for use of the computers, the teacher arranged things so they didn't have to. It was a great idea, but it didn't work. The boys' computers were in constant use, and the girls' stood idle. The longer the girls' computers went unused, the more their equipment seemed somehow inferior to the boys'—as if it somehow wasn't worth using.

The boys were going crazy as they watched two of the four workstations sit idle, and everyone knew something had to change. That's when the students came up with their own idea: any two, any time. Boys could use any free computer, but at any time girls in the class could bump them off until at least two computers were occupied by girls. "It took a couple of months, but over time the girls really relished the power they had to kick a boy off the computer," says Dr. Upitis. Sure, the boys would still run to grab one of the few available seats, but five minutes later, a girl knew that she could ask to jump in if there was something she wanted to do. It was just the kind of power play that girls this age enjoy. In a few months, the computer time was being used equally by the boys and girls in the classroom.[16]

Most classrooms, though, don't have the benefit of a researcher on site to point out inequities and help the teacher develop strategies for correcting them. More often than not, those inequities go unseen by the teacher and unchallenged by the students.

Teaching the Teachers

For twenty years Jo Sanders has been a tireless advocate for gender equity in math, science, and computer education. From 1990 to 1993 she coordinated the Computer Equity Expert Project, in which 200 educators—half of whom were computer teachers—participated in intensive gender equity training. Each teacher then went back to his or her school and worked with colleagues to raise awareness of equity issues and devise strategies for increasing girls' enrollment in math, science, and computer classes.

The results of the teachers' efforts were incredible. Once teachers became aware of the inequities, they almost immediately began to fashion strategies for increasing girls' participation. Here's just a sample of the gains achieved in less than one year. In one New York school, the ratio of girls to boys in the computer lab after school went from a dismal 2:25 to 1:1. In 1991 there were no girls in the computer science elective at an Oklahoma school. By the following year, thirty-one percent of the students enrolled in the class were girls. In one Virginia school, the Advanced Placement Pascal class started out with no girls enrolled. A year later, half the class was girls.

How did schools achieve these phenomenal results? Teachers and counselors invited girls to sign up for courses, rather than waiting for them to enroll on their own. They made a concerted effort to acknowledge girls' expertise and to use them as assistants. They changed course descriptions to focus on the end results, rather than the equipment being used. They employed 101 different techniques to entice girls to participate and to recognize their skills.

To the extent that teachers, parents, and educators are made aware of the issues, the problems are fairly easily solved, says Sanders. Too often, though, it's an invisible issue. There's no squeaky wheel demanding everyone's attention.

Equal Time

It's a hot October afternoon and every computer is taken in Jane Holzapfel's computer class. Today, the middle school students are continuing their unit on spreadsheets, this time learning how to create charts from the data they've entered.

As Ms. Holzapfel asks a question, several students raise their hands, a few call out the answer. The teacher calls on one of the students who sits waiting for a chance to share the answer with her classmates. "Good, Annie. You've got it," she says encouragingly. Later on she asks the students who can identify the X and Y axis on the graph, and once again hands start waving in the air. This time Ms. Holzapfel calls on Quyn. She answers correctly, and again the teacher responds with encouraging words. Throughout the class Ms. Holzapfel alternates between boys and girls, taking great pains to ask each of them a question and to give each an opportunity to respond to her inquiries.

Toward the end of each class, Ms. Holzapfel plays a short game with her students: she asks them questions based on the material they've gone over that day. Students who answer correctly get a piece of candy as a reward for their attentiveness. But Ms. Holzapfel doesn't rely on her own good intentions to ensure that girls and boys get an equal opportunity to play the game and win a prize. She uses a program that randomly generates a student's name from her class roster. No one—not even the teacher—knows whose name will come up next.

Holzapfel's interaction with her students is in marked contrast to what takes place in most classrooms today, where boys consistently receive the lion's share of the attention, are asked more challenging questions, and are encouraged to solve more complex problems. "The classroom consists of two worlds: one of boys in action, the other of girls inaction," wrote Myra and David Sadker in *Failing At Fairness: How America's Schools Cheat Girls*. "[Boys] get criticized. They get help when they are confused. They are the heart and center of interaction . . . girls receive less time, less help, and fewer challenges."[17]

Holzapfel credits a course she took in the summer of 1996 with opening her eyes to the many ways in which she favored boys in her classroom. The course, Girl-TECH, is sponsored by the Center for Research in Parallel Computation, a National Science Foundation-funded science and technology center headquartered at Rice University in Houston. Begun in 1995, the impetus behind GirlTECH is twofold: to train teachers in the ways of the World Wide Web and to raise their awareness about gender issues and computing. Each summer, twenty teachers spend two weeks on the Rice University campus. Here they learn how to use the Internet in their classrooms, how to publish their lesson plans on the Web for other teachers to use, and how to examine their teaching styles, their lesson plans, and their attitudes with an eye toward providing equity for the girls in their classes.

"It really opened my eyes," says the veteran teacher. "I've made a conscious effort to get more girls involved, to call on them more, to ask them to help me out when I need a student assistant." She's also begun to scrutinize her class assignments, and to seek out subjects that might appeal equally to boys and girls.

Programs such as GirlTECH or Sanders' Computer Equity Expert Project demonstrate what a tremendous impact teachers can have in undoing years of inequity in the classroom.

Unfortunately, though, the programs are still few in number—and most are limited to in-service classes for existing teachers. There is very little in the way of equity training in preservice teacher education, where it has the potential to affect every new teacher entering our classrooms.

Shining Examples

In the coming chapters you'll read about several schools that have developed strategies and designed programs that foster equitable participation among boys and girls. Their approaches are as different as the schools themselves, but they've all come up with a formula that has been successful in captivating girls' attention and involving them in both classroom and extracurricular activities.

The schools profiled in the coming pages aren't unique in trying to understand how to make computers accessible and relevant to all students, and their approaches are not the only way to achieve equitable computer use, but each, in its own way, has made a start: they've recognized the problem and started down the long road to solve it. And that, as they say, is half the battle.

6

No Boys Allowed

Cynthia Lanius remembers the precise moment she decided to start a girls-only technology club at Charles H. Milby High School in East Houston. She hit on the idea one fall day in 1996 during her tenth-grade geometry class. She'd lugged her notebook computer to school that day and on a whim decided to take a break from the regular classroom routine and dazzle her students with a tour of the Internet.

"How many of you would like to get on the Internet?" she asked her class, expecting to be bowled over by a throng of students charging to the front of the room. After all, the Web is hip. Pop and rap music stars have their own Web pages, as do hit TV shows, movies, even professional athletes. You can't go anywhere or read anything without seeing some reference to a new Web page. The kids will go nuts, she thought. And she was right. But only partly. Nine students rushed to her desk: eight boys and one girl. Although another teacher might not have even noticed the lack of interest among the girls, for Mrs. Lanius it was a disappointment and a worry. After all, these were *her girls* (as she affectionately refers to them). What could she do to pique their interest? she wondered. What could she do to show them what a vital, interesting resource the Web could be for them?

True to her word, she showed those first nine students some of her favorite Web sites: the Houston Rockets' and NBA homepages (she *loves* basketball), along with her own homepage, which features information about their high school, and (of course) her favorite math sites. But the whole time she was clicking from spot to spot, Mrs. Lanius was trying to figure out how she could bring more girls to the front of the room.

"Would any of you like to see Selena's homepage?" she asked all of a sudden, knowing that anything having to do with the Texas-born singing sensation, who was killed in 1995, was a surefire hit with her mostly Latina girls. Sure enough, the girls were soon pushing for a spot in front of the computer screen right along with the guys. "It was an in-my-face symbol of the different interests of girls and boys," recalls Mrs. Lanius. "Girls aren't as interested in technology for technology's sake. You have to find other ways to get them interested."

Find another way she did, and continues to do. Through a fellowship from the American Association of University Women (AAUW), Mrs. Lanius formed the Women's Technology Council at her high school. The young women meet every Tuesday evening from five to seven P.M in the school's cavernous computer lab. By day, the facility is packed with students practicing for a state assessment test. But by night, it's transformed into a sanctuary for Mrs. Lanius' girls—a place for them to learn, to play, to work. A place where they can discover the World Wide Web, improve their computer skills, and meet women who've pursued careers in technology-related fields. A place where no boys are allowed.

Making Up for Lost Time

It's 5:30 on a Tuesday evening and about two dozen girls are slowly filtering in to the computer lab at Milby High School. There's Myrna G., a smartly dressed senior who's come back to school after working all afternoon at an office downtown. She's tired and wants to go home so she can rest and grab some dinner before starting in on her homework, but she stopped by to check out the club nonetheless. The reason? "I want to major in computer engineering," she explains, "and Mrs. Lanius said it would be a good idea to come." Edna M. is a senior, too.

She's been at school since long before the bell rang for the first morning class. The technology council is one of several academic and social clubs she belongs to—all of which, she tells me, are necessary if she wants to get into a good college. Like Myrna, Edna has already put in a full day, but she enjoys the camaraderie the club affords. "I like the idea that it's just for girls. Guys think they can do more than girls. This shows that girls are interested, too," she proudly asserts.

The bond between Mrs. Lanius and her senior girls is unmistakable. Her devotion to them is indisputable: she teaches a special "makeup" calculus course before school for two girls whose jobs conflict with class time, started the technology club, and helps to organize Saturday seminars and field trips to expose girls to math, science, and technology-related subjects. They, in turn, are devoted to her. When asked why they joined the technology club, despite their already full schedules, each of the girls' response mentions Mrs. Lanius: "Mrs. Lanius said it was important for us," says one girl. "Mrs. Lanius said it would be a good idea," explains another. "Mrs. Lanius told us how we need to be good role models for the freshman girls," responds a third.

Every girl recognizes the value of improving her computer skills, but no one joined the Women's Technology Council just to learn how to surf the Web or how to maneuver in Windows 95. In fact, as I spoke with each of the girls, I couldn't help but wonder if they

would have participated in the club had it been organized by someone other than Mrs. Lanius. She's more
than just their math teacher. She's their role model, their
mentor, their friend.

Those of us who were fortunate enough to bond with
a teacher in school know just how important that relationship can be. The right teacher can unlock talents and
interests that we might otherwise never know existed, or
provide the support and encouragement we need to
tackle difficult subjects or pursue a less traditional path.
All students can benefit from such a relationship, but
girls in particular need to be associated with what the
AAUW in its report, *Growing Smart: What's Working
for Girls in School*, calls "caring adults." These are teachers or others "who will spend time with them, listen to
their ideas, and help them learn to stretch and excel."[18]
The bond between Mrs. Lanius and her students certainly fits that role. Mrs. Lanius thrives on her relationships with her students—and the girls, in turn, thrive
and excel as a result of her concern and attention.

Not long after we first spoke, Mrs. Lanius sent me a
copy of an electronic mail message she'd received from
one of her girls. The message was a source of intrigue,
since the student had sent it using just a screen name,
promising mysteriously to identify herself at graduation.

*"Well I just wanted to say that I look up to you, and
I think you're a great teacher. I'm sure you have no*

idea who I am so I'll let you figure that one out. Let's see if you are as good in solving mysteries as you are in math. . . ."

Mrs. Lanius was thrilled by the message—personally and professionally. Connecting in a personal way with any student—making a difference to them—makes all the nights and weekends she puts in worthwhile. But she was particularly thrilled that one of her girls was using e-mail as the medium to tell her how much she meant.

Long Days, Late Nights

Life isn't easy for Mrs. Lanius' girls. They get up well before dawn and go to bed long after David Letterman has signed off for the night. They take a full load of honors classes, participate in half a dozen academic societies, and hold down jobs inside and out of their homes. Many come from immigrant families. None are what could be considered privileged, or even middle class. Some will be the first in their families to graduate from high school. Most will be the first to graduate from college. Although one or two of the girls have access to a computer at home, or at a relative's house, most of their families haven't been able to afford a personal computer.

These girls are on a mission. They're on their way to becoming doctors, engineers, biologists, and computer

scientists. Although they're just sixteen and seventeen, they act mature beyond their years. Their senior year of school isn't only about proms and homecoming games. It's about applying for college, taking Advanced Placement tests, working a part-time job, and coming to school at 7:30 A.M. to make up for the in-class time they miss while working downtown. But as hard as these girls have worked (most have taken four years of honors math and science classes), they've typically taken only one high school computer course. And, since many of the girls don't have computers at home, they're getting ready to enter college without the basic skills now expected of first-year students.

"I'm concerned for them," Mrs. Lanius says of her senior girls. "They're going to be walking into courses where computer knowledge is required and they're all scared that they aren't ready." That's why she started the technology council, and why she takes advantage of every opportunity to get their hands on the keyboard, their faces in front of a computer monitor. She's recommended several of her female students for a two-week summer program at neighboring Rice University. During that time, students learn to use the Internet as a research tool, are coached in how to write an effective essay for a college entrance application, and spend time with mentors who show them what college life is all about.

For Amanda S., now a high school senior with her sights squarely set on college, the two weeks were a

wake-up call. "I didn't know as much as some of the other students," she recalls, either about computers in general or the Internet specifically. Amanda is lucky, though. She discovered the deficiencies in the relatively protected environment of a summer program. She still had her senior year (and Mrs. Lanius' help) to get up to speed on computers and the Internet. Imagine how much worse it would have been for her to discover as a freshman in college that she was lacking the basic computer skills expected of incoming students—the skills that most of her classmates already possessed.

Mrs. Lanius later tells me that her students had always worked on Windows computers and were, for the first time, introduced to Macintosh computers at the summer program. "Here come the other students, they sit right down and go like trailblazers. For our students, the difference between Macintosh and Windows computers was just enough to be bothersome to them," she says. If she'd known, says Mrs. Lanius, she would have given the students a tutorial in Macintosh basics ahead of time. No one thought of that, though, exacerbating even further the students' lack of computer skills.

For the senior girls, summer programs and weekly meetings of the technology council won't be enough to put them on a par with many of their future classmates— particularly the girls who intend to major in computer engineering or computer science—but it's a start. And for the freshman and sophomore girls, the technology

council, and the hands-on experience it affords, may be what it takes to get them interested in higher-level computer courses—so they won't be in the position of having to play catch-up later on.

For the Girls

Technology and computer clubs are not new to schools. Since early-model personal computers were introduced to schools in the 1980s, small groups of students have hung out after school or during lunch and recess to play games, work on computer programs, and participate in contests. But those small groups of "techies" have almost always been boys (though interestingly, the advisors are often women).[19] Although the focus of computer clubs and the faces of their participants are slowly changing, they have long been largely the domain of boys and young men.

Until recently, that is.

Throughout the United States, in elementary through high schools, teachers like Mrs. Lanius are establishing technology and computer clubs just for girls. The focus of these clubs varies, depending upon the age and the needs of the participants. In some high schools, for example, the clubs provide mentoring and support for girls interested in pursuing computer-related careers. In others, the activities are more remedial, designed to improve upon the computer skills of the participants. Elementary and middle school clubs tend to focus on encouraging girls to explore and experiment. At the high school level, they are more geared toward career interests and mentoring. At every level, though, the clubs are designed to build young women's confidence and instill in them the belief that computers are as much for them as they are for the boys.

During the 1996–1997 academic year, I visited four schools with girls-only computer clubs and spoke with participants in similar programs from St. Louis, Missouri, to the San Francisco Bay Area. I sat in on meetings, tagged along on field trips, and spoke to participating teachers and students about their plans, their hopes, and their frustrations. I discovered that each of these clubs was born out of the same general desire to broaden girls' exposure to computer-related activities. Cynthia Lanius started the Women's Technology Council as a crash course to get her senior girls up to speed in the technology that would be an integral part of their college lives. Halfway across the country in Union City, California, elementary school teacher Cathaleen Hampton established an after-school computer academy to cultivate leadership skills in third- and fourth-grade girls. And near Arimo, Idaho, a rural area outside Pocatello, the Young Women in Technology Workshop began out of a desire to bolster girls' enrollment in vocational technology classes.

These clubs are about cooperation, not competition,

about working together on group projects—or helping each other out on individual assignments, not racing to see who can finish a project first. They're about developing girls' excitement, abilities, and confidence, on the computer and off.

Tomorrow's Leaders Today

While Cynthia Lanius is helping her girls develop the computer skills they'll need in college, Cathaleen Hampton is laying the groundwork so that her third- and fourth-grade girls at Alvarado Elementary School won't need to scramble later on.

Her kindergarten through fourth grade school is located in Union City, California. It has an ethnically diverse population, with a high percentage of students for whom English is not the native language. One testimony to the school's diversity is its homepage on the World Wide Web, which provides information in many languages including Spanish, Tagalog, Farsi, Hindi, and Vietnamese. Many of the students come from extremely traditional families, where the young girls are given many of the household responsibilities: they take care of younger brothers and sisters, pick up things around the house, cook the family meals. And although the school is technologically rich (proceeds from a special property tax have paid for equipment and training), many of the families are quite poor. Home computers are a luxury few can afford.

Mrs. Hampton, a third-grade classroom teacher and a self-taught computer junkie, started the Computer Academy in the spring of 1994. The girls meet Tuesday afternoons in the school's computer lab to explore new software, create their own Web pages, and learn to be eager, self-sufficient computer users. The goal, says Mrs. Hampton, is to get the girls hooked on computers—as tools and as toys—to bolster their confidence before they reach the middle-school years.

When I met Mrs. Hampton, the academy was just beginning its third year. Although there'd been some fits and starts getting the program off the ground, they'd already had some important successes. Girls who participated in the program were recognized around the school as technology leaders. They were the first to explore the Internet, the first to experiment with new software tools; they were even given the password to move or save files on the computer—a privilege never before afforded to students. Along the way they were gaining confidence in their computer skills—and in themselves.

Nadia's Story

When she entered the Computer Academy in third grade, things weren't looking so great for nine-year-old Nadia D. The daughter of two migrant farm workers, she'd moved to California from Mexico when she was four. She was shy, and unsure of herself. She was having difficulty with reading. She rarely participated in class. She was, says Mrs. Hampton, the perfect candidate for the Computer Academy. "We don't necessarily pick the leaders," she explains. "We look for students who'll benefit from developing those skills."

At first, Nadia showed the same timidity in the after-school program that she had in class. She wouldn't make a move without first asking if it was okay. And then, something remarkable happened. Nadia, along with the other girls in the Computer Academy, discovered the Internet. They were the first group in the school to explore the World Wide Web using the school's new high-speed connection. They were in a privileged position and they knew it.

"All of a sudden they were off," recalls Mrs. Hampton. They started sharing information with each other, showing each other interesting sites. And Nadia was at the front of the group. She got so excited, in fact, that she volunteered to demonstrate the Internet to her class. "She stood there and showed the whole class how to get onto the Internet," says Mrs. Hampton. "It was phenomenal!"

Nadia, like some of the other girls in the Computer Academy, is now the technical guru for her class—but the metamorphosis didn't happen overnight. Nadia worked hard to overcome her initial shyness and hesitancy at the computer, and she did it with the help of two of her teachers—Mrs. Hampton, and her classroom teacher—both of whom saw that beneath Nadia's quiet, tentative exterior was a bright, eager girl just waiting to come out.

"HELP!"

With a computer lab filled with twenty or more children, problems at the computer can quickly turn into a free-for-all of waving hands and cries of "Help me! Help me!" That's why Mrs. Hampton and her associates developed a visual cue to let them know who needed assistance. Sitting on top of each Macintosh computer are two cups, one red and one yellow. Their bases are taped together, forming something of an hour-glass shape. When the yellow cup is on top, the teachers know that everything's fine. When students need help, they flip the cups over so the red cup is on top. The system works perfectly. It cuts down on noise and frantic arm motions. Yet even a perfectly devised system like this one can be used as a crutch, as Mrs. Hampton soon discovered.

One afternoon, during one of the first sessions of the Computer Academy, Mrs. Hampton decided to start the day's session off with an experiment: she unplugged all the computers before the girls arrived. It would be up to the students to identify and correct the problem—a first step on their road to self-sufficiency. As the girls filed in, their teacher stood back, watched, and waited. One by one the girls sat down at a computer, only to discover that it wouldn't turn on. It wouldn't do anything. For a brief moment they were horrified and flustered, and then each one promptly did what she'd been taught to do: she flipped over the cups so the red cup was on top. She asked her teacher for help. This time, though, Mrs. Hampton had only questions—no answers—for the girls. "What are you going to do?" she asked each of them. "What do you think might be wrong?" It took the whole session—forty agonizing minutes—for each of the girls to realize that the computers were unplugged. But by the end, they'd all figured it out, and the cups were flipped back on the "everything's okay" yellow side.

"How many times do we step in to rescue a girl versus a boy? They don't ever get time to figure it out. I forced them to confront what was holding them back," asserts Mrs. Hampton triumphantly.

Something pretty incredible happened in the forty minutes it took the girls to get their computers working again. Sure, they were frustrated and annoyed. But by the time they left they were empowered. They knew that they had diagnosed and corrected the problem. And that knowledge was a powerful thing.

The lesson worked so well that Mrs. Hampton repeated it when a new group of girls entered the computer academy the following year. Just to keep things interesting (she had six returning girls that year), she unplugged the power cords *and* the mice, once again leaving it to the girls to diagnose and correct the problem. This time, Nadia and the other second-year girls didn't miss a beat. After a few minutes of tinkering, they were up and running. All the girls were eager to help their friends out, but Mrs. Hampton didn't let them.

The newcomers, like the veterans, needed to realize they could figure it out for themselves.

Where Are All the Girls?

To the casual observer, Mischell Anderson and Mary Lou Oslund don't have a lot in common. Mischell teaches at a large high school in the San Francisco Bay Area. Her classes look like break-out groups from the United Nations general assembly, with African American students sitting alongside Filipinos, Hispanics, and Caucasian students. Mary Lou teaches in a small high school in rural Idaho. Her students are almost exclusively white and few have ventured farther than nearby Pocatello. Mischell Anderson teaches social studies and multimedia. Mary Lou Oslund teaches photography, drafting, and other vocational technology courses. Both, however, have a fervent belief in the need for role models to advance and nurture girls' interest in technology—and both started programs that turned those beliefs into reality.

Why Bother?

Five girls. That's how many female students were enrolled in all of Mary Lou Oslund's vocational technology classes. Although the drafting, digital photography, and yearbook courses were popular with the boys, she noticed that the girls weren't exactly beating down the doors to get in. And why should they? For most of the girls at her rural Idaho high school, the skills learned in the high-tech classes had no relationship to their lives. Many of the girls got married and began raising a family right after high school. Few went on to college or to vocational training programs. What good were desktop publishing skills or expertise in computer-aided design if your career in life was going to be raising children? "I realized," says Mrs. Oslund, "that I needed to show the women students that there was something for them at the end of these classes. That they could do something with the skills they'd be learning."

That's why she organized her first Young Women in Technology Workshop, an extracurricular program for girls in ninth through twelfth grade. Working with other teachers, she identified a group of girls who would benefit from a program of self-esteem building and career counseling. That was in the fall of 1990. Since that time, nearly sixty young women—more than half of her school's female population—have participated. Each year, participating students attend after-school seminars in self-esteem building and career planning, including presentations by local professional women. They also participate in several day-long field trips to area businesses— from a computer chip manufacturer to the regional FBI office—to get a firsthand glimpse at the many ways in which technology is used in the workplace.

In her own quiet way, Mrs. Oslund is doing much more than simply trying to increase the number of women in her classes. Through her seminars and field trips, she is showing the young women in her school that they have options. By introducing them to women who own their own businesses or who have successful careers in technology-driven fields, she is providing them with tangible examples of the many ways in which they might use the technical skills taught in her classes. Even if the young women do not choose to go into one of these professions right after high school, says Mrs. Oslund, "I tell them that sometime down the road they may need to support a family and they can fall back on skills they've learned."

You have to look no further than Mrs. Oslund's classes to see the dramatic impact her program has had. During Vocational Education Week of the 1996–1997 school year, four students received recognition for their outstanding work: all four were young women. Several graduates have gone on to take more advanced courses in college or pursue a technical trade. And in all but one of Mrs. Oslund's courses, there's an equal representation of young men and women. Her drafting course, the last all-male bastion, now has ten young women enrolled. It's not quite an equal representation, but it's a start.

Mischell Anderson saw the same disturbing trend

when she surveyed her multimedia classes at the start of the 1996–1997 school year. Only seven young women were enrolled in the elective course. While Ms. Anderson was trying to figure out why girls weren't signing up for the classes, she came across a news article about a group of women in San Francisco who were starting a mentoring program for high school women. What a great fit, she thought, and quickly called the local chapter of Webgrrls (part of a national organization for women in Web-related businesses). Out of that phone call Techgirls was created, a mentoring program for high school women. "I want to encourage girls who have an interest in technology," says Anderson. "I want to show them how many women are involved in the field." To that end, each girl corresponds (by e-mail, of course) with at least one woman in a high-tech career. They can ask questions about their mentor's experiences, query them about classes they think they should take, or share their concerns about being a young woman interested in a field that is still dominated by men. The mentoring and modeling doesn't stop with e-mail. The Techgirls have visited HotWired and Salon, two online magazines with a large contingent of women editors; they've spent the day at the computer science department at the University of California at Berkeley and had lunch with the women graduate students; they've chatted online with NASA scientists, and spent time exploring online sites for girls and young women.

Techgirl Extraordinaire

Nicole M. didn't need to attend a Techgirls meeting to get her psyched about working with computers. She's one of nine girls in her Multimedia II class and plans on enrolling in Multimedia III next semester—where she expects there'll be even fewer female faces.

When we met, Nicole was working with another student to develop the club's Web pages—and was clearly enjoying the effort. "Check out these backgrounds," she tells some of the other club members. "Me and Marguerite found a ton of them on the Web."

Nicole is one of the Techgirls regulars and has tried to convince her less techie friends to join. "Some girls say they're too dumb. Others think it's too nerdy," she explains. "I used to be one of those people—until I took the multimedia course." That's when she discovered computer design. Working with another student she profiled a day in the life of a high school student (who just happened to be one of her best friends). The results of their work are featured for the world to see in the school's homepage.

For Nicole, Techgirls is a place to go for encouragement—explicit and implicit—to keep her motivated, even though she is one of so few young women in her program. For other young women, though, the club fills an even more basic need, says Ms. Anderson. "My biggest goal is to expand the girls' imaginations. They can only achieve in life as much as they imagine themselves doing. If they don't see women in high-tech careers, they'll never be able to imagine themselves in those positions either."

Only a Beginning

Without exception, every girl I spoke with—from third graders to high school seniors, novices to pros—valued the girls-only environment and believed that allowing boys in their program would dilute its purpose. Susie M., a senior in Cynthia Lanius' Women's Technology Council in Houston, had clearly given the issue some thought. She observes, "When I was a sophomore, there was a boy in geometry class who always knew how to solve the problems. Everyone always asked him for help. We need to learn this stuff ourselves. We can't always depend on someone else."

Each of these programs has had a profound impact on the participating girls. Stories such as Nadia's or Nicole's are a testament to the power of a dedicated teacher and a strong program to make a difference. But these programs also raise some very difficult issues for parents, teachers, and students alike.

Too often, single-gender programs of any type are considered inferior to the regular programs. Although coordinators of girls' computer clubs take great pains to keep their programs from being labeled "remedial," it's a distinction that's hard to avoid—and one that can wind up thwarting the efforts to boost the confidence of the participants.

And what about the girls who don't participate in these programs? By their very nature, the programs are voluntary. While each of the teachers has tried to reach out to a broad population of girls at her school, inevitably some of the girls who would benefit most from the supportive environment and the opportunity to learn new technical skills never get involved.

There's also a very real danger that the clubs will take the attention away from the long-term, systematic changes that are necessary if schools are to provide girls with the opportunities they deserve. Cynthia Lanius knows that, and is working to add an additional computer science course to the required curriculum for all students. Cathy Hampton is working with other teachers to try to raise their awareness of gender issues inside the classroom. Mischell Anderson, working with other social science teachers at her high school, is actively incorporating technology into a wide range of classes, so that even the young women who don't take technology classes will benefit from a rich exposure to CD-ROM and Internet-based resources. For her part, Mary Lou Oslund is witnessing profound changes in classroom dynamics as more women enroll in her courses. "It brings an extra dimension to anything we're studying," she says.

As gender equity specialist Jo Sanders sees it, single-gender programs are "short-term smart; long-term stupid." They can't be viewed as "the answer" to inequities between boys and girls. They are an important part, but only part of the solution to the disparity in both the knowledge and confidence level of boys and girls. Fundamental, long-lasting changes will only occur when we rethink what goes on every day in coed classrooms throughout the country, where the vast majority of boys and girls alike receive their education.

7

From Dance Schools to Web Design

Coed Programs That Work for Girls and Boys

Sixth-grade teacher Kathleen Bridgewater has spent a great deal of time thinking about how to plan lessons using the computer. She understands the power of the technology to expand ideas and enhance classroom learning—or to shut students out if the lessons aren't carefully designed and implemented. That's why she strives to find topics that are both girl- and boy-friendly. And that's why, when she was preparing a geometry lesson using the Logo programming language in Microworlds Project Builder, she chose a dance school metaphor. Using the popular software, the students write commands that control a small turtle's movements on the screen. Ms. B's Turtle School of Dance, as the lesson is aptly called, has been effective in piquing the girls' interest—in math and in computers.

Applying the lessons they've learned in geometry class, the students program their turtles to glide about the computer screen tracing regular polygons. "Our work goes beyond the typical categorizing of angles in an elementary curriculum," explains Ms. Bridgewater. Using a combination of the ClarisWorks spreadsheet and Microworlds Project Builder, the children analyze patterned changes in the sizes of interior angles as each side is added. As they program the turtle to "Square Dance" or to do the "Pentagon Polka" students draw on concepts such as supplementary angles to determine what turns must be programmed.

This is serious math, but it's also a lot of fun. The last in the series of lessons requires students to program an animated dance school recital in which all the polygon dances are displayed. The theme especially seems to intrigue girls, who become more computer savvy as they try to imitate real-life recitals, complete with Logo electronic music, narration, and recorded applause. Explains Ms. Bridgewater: "The challenge of problem-solving ensures everyone's intense participation," adding, "For gender equity it helps that we have a sufficient number of computers so each student runs his or her own program. In this way, dominant personalities are not stifling the development of skills in others."

Ms. Bridgewater teaches at Erving Elementary

School in a small industrial New England town where there are only 170 students in kindergarten through sixth grade. Although the median income of the town is just $30,000, the school and the larger community have made a commitment to technology that rivals that of many more affluent areas. When I visited, the school was four years into a comprehensive five-year technology plan that has required the commitment and support of the whole community: students, teachers, parents, and some area business owners. Through a combination of grants, regular funds, and generous contributions from the town government, as well as area businesses, in a few short years students have gone from using old Apple IIe's (built in the 1980s) to working on Macintoshes that are connected to one another and to the Internet. The commitment stems from a belief in the critical role that computer skills will play in the lives of area children, but everyone in the community is potentially benefiting from the investment in technology: the school's lab is open three nights a week so that area residents—adults and children alike—can use the facility for work and for play.

It stands to reason that such a community would have an unconventional school. From the minute I walked in the front door of the building, I sensed there was something different about this school. The rectangular-shaped building was built in the seventies when the "schools without walls" fad was all the rage. The classes are small—there are rarely more than twenty students for every teacher—and the classroom walls are easily dismantled and resituated as the need arises. At the heart of the building—literally and conceptually—are the school's two media centers: the library and the computer lab. The library stretches over one whole wing, located adjacent to the primary grades. The computer lab is in a large open space (there are no traditional hallways here), just outside the third-, fourth-, fifth-, and sixth-grade classrooms.

Computers are as much a part of the education experience here as books or other learning materials. As with most schools, teachers sign up to use the seventeen-computer lab throughout the school day, typically from thirty to forty minutes at a time. But what sets this school apart from many others throughout the country is that lab time isn't about "doing computers," or engaging in activities with little to no relevance to the teaching that's going on in the classroom. Quite the contrary. The lab is both physically and academically an extension of the classroom. Teachers lead the computer activities, which are generally tightly woven into their lesson plans.

Technology integration specialist Michael Lipinski (M.L. to his students) taught fifth and sixth grade for twenty years before becoming the school's full-time computer guru. He works closely with the classroom teachers to design computer activities that are a natural progression of what's going on in the classroom. So third- and fourth-graders, for example, put the theories they've learned in the simple machines units of their science class into practice by creating Rube Goldberg-type devices using a software program called the Incredible Machine. Fifth and sixth graders log on to weather sites on the Internet during their study of weather patterns in science class and create an online business directory for the town, designing Web pages for the same businesses that employ many of their mothers and their fathers. And students at all grade levels use the computers to refine and illustrate everything from essays to poems to short stories.

Although students are sometimes grouped in pairs or teams when the project will benefit from collaboration, most of the time, when the students sit down to begin a new activity, they each do so at their own computer. There's no pushing and shoving, no question of whose hand is going to be on the mouse guiding the activities, and really learning the lesson. With each new activity, boys and girls alike grow more comfortable with the tools and increase their understanding of the many ways computers can be used to solve everyday problems.

Computer time doesn't stop when the class period ends. Massachusetts winters can be long and harsh, so the lab is open before school, during recess and lunch, and after school. On inclement days, the seventeen Macintoshes are humming away—with girls, as well as boys, rushing to get a place at the screen. The easy access and integrated lessons have paid off for all students, but have been particularly beneficial to the girls, who show just as much excitement and interest in the technology as the boys—both in and out of class.

Clearly, Michael Lipinski is one of the reasons students enjoy computer time as much as they do. His lessons are engaging and challenging, and his penchant for coming up with fun extracurricular activities has turned participating in after-school computing projects into a privilege—something that both boys and girls aspire to. In the fall of 1996, when he first heard about CyberSurfari, an Internet treasure hunt for elementary school students sponsored by several Web-based businesses, he immediately put the word out that he was looking for volunteers. Working in teams, students would be answering questions and solving puzzles in order to find seventy-five out of one hundred hidden treasures located on Web sites around the world. "We were pretty serious about winning, so it was going to be pretty intense—lots of after-school time," says Lipinski. He wound up with enough students to form three teams—and more than half of the volunteers were girls.

At eleven years old, Kim N. is already becoming something of an Internet veteran. She's created two Web pages for area businesses and was part of the school's winning CyberSurfari team. Exactly twenty-four hours after the contest began (and after ten hours of online time), her group found its seventy-fifth Web site treasure.

"I just like doing things on the computer," says Kim. "At home I do homework or play games. If we had the Internet I'd do that, too, but we don't. That's what I like here. We have a chance to explore." Her penchant for exploration has paid off. She and her team wound up finding eighty-three of one hundred hidden Internet treasures faster than just about any other team of students in the country: one clue, one puzzle at a time.

The school's homepage on the World Wide Web proudly features a picture of their winning CyberSurfari team grinning from ear to ear for the whole world to see—the girls right alongside the boys.

A School Within a School

Networked computers and Internet access are fairly recent additions to most schools—even those in fairly affluent areas. However, at the Ralph Bunche School in Harlem, where many of the mostly Latino and African American students live in neighboring housing projects, students and teachers have been using sophisticated computer equipment since the late 1980s. That's when the staff was invited to participate in a cutting-edge research project. The school-wide experiment was designed to investigate what would happen if students, teachers, and administrators had access to network computers much like those used by scientists for collaborative study. How would the technology change the way students learned? The way teachers taught? The way the entire school community interacted with one another?

The introduction of networked computers was the catalyst for a dramatic change in the business of education at this school. Using their newfound tools, teachers and students began to work collaboratively on many projects. Students took increasingly more responsibility for their work, storing assignments in individual and classroom workspaces on the networked computers. Teachers, for their part, used the workspaces for projects that they repeated with each new class, providing for greater consistency and continuity in their approach.

The experiment worked so well, in fact, that in 1990 a small group of teachers proposed to extend the experiment even further—to start a Computer Mini-School for fourth, fifth, and sixth graders (selected by lottery from among all applicants), where technology would be integrated into all aspects of the curriculum. The Mini-School would attempt to fully incorporate technology into education reform—reform that included, among other things, smaller class sizes and fewer pull-out programs, in which students are pulled from classes for remedial help.

Here in this "school within a school," every student attends a computer lab twice a week and has an e-mail account and unfettered access to the Internet (for everything from researching reports to downloading sound-bytes of the latest hit single). It's a school where students' work is regularly published on the Internet. And it's a school where a group of dedicated sixth-grade girls put out a newspaper chronicling the life and times of students, faculty, and area residents.

All the News . . .

The school newspaper, "written and published several times a year by students," wasn't started as a girls-only activity, but it's been staffed by mostly girls for as long as advisor Mona Monroe can remember. Mrs. Monroe, who retired after teaching at the school for thirty-five years, comes several afternoons a week to help get the paper out. She's a sometimes coach, sometimes teacher, sometimes confidante, and always a fierce advocate for the girls at the Computer Mini-School.

Although it wasn't devised as such, the paper has been largely a female endeavor, says Mrs. Monroe. "Except for that one year, when we had a bunch of boys who loved to do anything on the computer. For the most part, though, it's the kind of activity girls enjoy and are good at," she attests.

As for the girls, they have their own theories about why so few boys have helped get the paper out over the years. "They're lazy," says one of the female staffers of the boys who choose not to work on the newspaper. "They don't want the responsibility."

Nicole W. is a little more thoughtful about it and

wonders aloud if the reason boys don't sign up for the newspaper staff is because it's full of girls (an ironic twist on the way the preponderance of adolescent boys can often deter a girl from joining a computer or technical club). "If there were a group of boys," she muses, "and the leader worked on the paper, the rest would follow."

Another editor shakes her head, agreeing with Nicole. "Maybe the boys won't want to do it because the girls can do something the boys can't. Say the boys don't know something the girls know and the girl says, 'I'll help you.' A lot of boys think girls can't help them."

One of her classmates and fellow editors nods in agreement. "It happens."

Each of the theories probably has a kernel of truth to it. At twelve years old, the girls are more involved in school than their male classmates, and more willing to devote the time and effort required to publish a newspaper. Sure, they have fun, but they also work hard—often to the exclusion of other activities. Being on the newspaper staff requires a level of responsibility that many of the boys aren't yet ready for. And, now that the staff is all girls, many boys do feel the same discomfort of joining that a girl their age feels walking into a room full of boys.

Most of the girls on staff are in sixth grade. They work on the paper after school several days a week, selecting stories from among the many submissions received from students (by e-mail, of course), taking photos around the school using a digital camera, and laying out the stories and putting them on the school's Web page.

"It's an advantage," says one of the editors matter-of-factly when I ask her what she thinks of being on the newspaper staff. "We learn a lot of things that most kids our age don't know much about. We learn a lot of stuff to prepare us for life—*if* any of us choose to go that route."

Whether "that route" turns out to be writing or editing, banking or science, the skills these girls are learning today provide a strong foundation on which to build. There is no hint of hesitancy or tentativeness at the computer, no shyness when it comes to exploring—whether it's a new tool or a new Web site. That confidence propels them into a range of technology-rich activities: several of them are members of a student video production team that chronicles events around school, they've attended local, state, and national education conferences to discuss their computer-related activities, and they know more about computers—and are more comfortable with the tools—than many of their older relatives.

But their proficiency didn't happen overnight. The girls on the newspaper, like all the students here, are immersed in technology from the minute they enter the Computer Mini-School. The school's two labs are open from eight in the morning until six at night when Technology Supervisor Paul Reese—the lifeblood of the organization—usually runs out of steam and decides to head home. Every writing assignment is done on the computer. "Everything we write has to be at least two hundred and fifty words," explains one fifth-grade girl who is also an after-school regular at the computer lab. "They won't accept anything less." As the students' writing skills improve—and as they grow more comfortable with the tools—they'll add pictures and diagrams to the written word. They hold "virtual" debates with other schools using video-conferencing hardware and software; they involve the whole world in probability experiments through their "Great Penny Toss" project; and they converse with children and adults from all over the country and around the world.

"We expect students to see the computer as a tool, as an avenue for communication," says Mr. Reese. "But it's also about developing an understanding of how to work collaboratively, how to be involved in an activity that is increasingly complex over time."

How does this approach benefit girls? Because everyone—from the shyest child, who starts out afraid to even touch the mouse, to the most aggressive student, who will take every opportunity to work and play on the computer—is afforded the same opportunities and is evaluated based on the same set of expectations. As with Erving Elementary School, access simply isn't an issue, so there isn't the danger of the most aggressive students (often, though not always, the boys) getting more than their share of time at the computer.

When the school first opened, says Mr. Reese, he and the other teachers knew that if left unchecked, the boys might take over the computer room. "We made sure that didn't happen, and once the tradition got started there's been no battle to fight. Once you get girls started, they take care of themselves," he adds.

There was a time, says teacher Ellen Clare, when it was always the boys asking, "Miss Clare, can I go down to play the computer?" The girls, she says, were more likely to read books or work on projects in the classroom during recess and lunch. Now, Ms. Clare is a traditional-ist who firmly believes in the importance of fundamen-tals, so she wasn't about to discourage girls from their reading activities. But she also recognizes the value of computer skills. That's why she found a way to get girls on the computer early and often, while still encouraging other interests.

"Every time the girls read a new story, or build some new construction, they are eager to tell me all about it. Now I tell them don't talk to me about it. Put it in writ-ing." And of course each of those writing assignments is done on the computer.

Perhaps most importantly, the computer work has meaning for the students. Their writing assignments in-volve discussing how they celebrate holidays with their families, or writing to the mayor of New York City about the plight of the homeless. They hone their online com-munications skills by sending e-mail to R. L. Stine, au-

thor of the wildly popular Goosebumps books. They become desktop publishing mavens by recounting mile-
stones in the history of the school and the community. In
short, among its many uses, the computer is their vehicle for sharing their opinions, hopes, and dreams with
the rest of the world.

An Elite Corps

In the two previous examples, girls thrived because of
school-wide efforts to be inclusive and through lessons
and activities that appeal to all students—male and female, shy and aggressive. At a middle school in the Mid-
west two very dedicated teachers have managed to apply
those same principles to a small, highly technical class—
a class that could just as easily be filled with a roomful of
boys.

When I read about Greenwood Middle School's Top
Gun program on the World Wide Web, I thought,
*Great. Another club where a bunch of guys play around
with computers.* With a name like Top Gun what else
could it be, right? Wrong. Although the name conjures
up images of Tom Cruise and his flyboy cronies, the program itself has none of those macho overtones. Quite
the contrary. Through the careful selection of participants and a commitment to pursuing topics that will appeal to adolescent boys and girls, Top Gun classes are a
place where participants of both sexes are able to use

state-of-the-art technology to explore a wide range of subjects.

As the name implies, students in the Top Gun program represent an elite squad. Although children can request to join the class, most participants are handpicked by their fourth grade teachers, based on their problem-solving abilities. Although the program is completely voluntary, it boasts a fairly equal representation of boys and girls. The reason? Encouragement from parents is certainly part of it. I heard a lot of, "Mom and Dad thought it would be a good idea," when I asked girls why they entered the program. Another critical factor, though, is timing. Although the Top Gun program is for middle-school students, for a variety of administrative reasons the participants are selected at the end of their fourth-grade year—before they get to middle school and are bombarded by conflicting academic and social demands. Once in the program, boys and girls alike tend to stay in. Only three students have dropped out of Top Gun since it was started in 1986: two boys and one girl.

Where Art Meets Technology

Outside it's nearing the end of 1996, but inside the Top Gun classroom it's 1860 all over again as students are hard at work preparing multimedia presentations on the Civil War. They've split up into pairs, with each team taking a different topic. Throughout the room, the students sit huddled in front of computer monitors, tweaking pictures to achieve the perfect look or moving text around so it's just right. At one table, two girls are developing a presentation on Civil War uniforms. The opening screen is divided in half. On one side is a Confederate soldier; on the other, a soldier from the Union army. Each is in full dress uniform. Deanna M. and Alexandra K. are researching battlefields; Crystal M. (who's working on her own today) chose Civil War etiquette for her area of study.

In one corner of the room, Karey J. is working alone today, too. Her partner is out sick, so she is trying to get through as much of the presentation as she can. Her topic is battles of the Civil War. Although she doesn't seem particularly enamored with the subject, as we sit and talk about the class, Karey slowly starts to share with me what she likes about being part of Top Gun.

"It's pretty fun. You get to know a lot more than anyone else does about computers. They even tell us the password for all the computers. We'd get kicked out if we ever told it to anyone who wasn't in the program," explains Karey, obviously pleased with having been entrusted with the top-secret information. "Plus, you get to work on projects—and you can talk while you work," she adds.

Projects. Working in pairs. Talking with your classmates. Those are all a big part of Top Gun—and a big reason the girls enjoy the program so much. Top Gun isn't about creating abstract programs, or individual variations on popular computer games. It's about developing dynamic yet practical presentations for their school and their broader community. First-time Top Gunners start by creating a presentation on the topic they know best: themselves. They quickly move on from there, starting with relatively simple projects such as a computer-based tour of the school (a project the sixth graders in the program were working on when I visited) to increasingly complex assignments: tours of the Indianapolis Art Museum and Conner Prairie, the first settlement in Indiana. More recently, the seventh-grade students completed a cyber tour of the Indianapolis Zoo, which is featured on the school's Web page. With a click of the mouse, visitors can browse pictures and read about the animals—from the emu (native to the Australian Plains) to the zebra finch, which is part of the zoo's Desert Biome exhibit.

The tour of the zoo, like every Top Gun project, required two distinct but complementary sets of skills: social skills—projects typically require extensive interviewing of experts—and technical skills, as students need to learn new programs and techniques to create sophisticated presentations. It's a balance that program creator Joe Huber believes is critical to creating computer-based projects that will appeal to both boys and girls. So instead of having students just "hack away," he looks for projects that require creativity and interpersonal interaction, projects that lean toward practical examples rather than abstract use of tools.

"It's Like a Bunch of Big Toys"

Of course, the best way to evaluate a program's success is to study its graduates. When I met Jamie F. she had already graduated from middle school and was nearing the end of her first term as a high school freshman. Unlike many girls her age, there was nothing tentative or uncertain about her. Although she was one of the younger girls in the group I met with, she was the first to introduce herself and couldn't keep from jumping in to add an additional point or two when one of her fellow Top Gun graduates was telling me about her experience in the program.

Was her participation in Top Gun the reason for Jamie's poise and confidence? "It helped big time," Jamie told me, laughing as she recalled the nervous girl who started the program in sixth grade. "I was really afraid when I started in the class. Most of the kids were in the gifted classes and I felt really stupid because I wasn't. I was so nervous that I sat next to another girl and kept asking her questions any time I couldn't figure something out. Then one day, she was sick and I was like, 'Oh, what should I do.' Finally, I started just looking at it and figuring things out. Little by little I started to relax."

As Top Gun eighth graders, Jamie and her classmate

Jennifer H. were responsible for creating a multimedia tutorial for the Indianapolis Art Museum. The two girls spent weeks studying the artwork, talking with the museum's education director, and writing up their own descriptions of the paintings and sculptures before ever sitting down to create their presentation on the computer. When the semester ended, the course was over, but the project wasn't complete. So Jamie and Jennifer arrived at school early, stayed in at recess and lunch, and hung out after school for several weeks until the project was finished.

Every graduate of the program I spoke with was extraordinarily confident in her abilities and eager to experiment with all kinds of technology. The girls in Top Gun, more than in any of the other programs or schools I observed, exhibited a trait rarely found in adolescent girls: unbridled enthusiasm for the technology. These girls weren't just coasting along because the skills would help them in their schoolwork, or because they wanted to get a good grade in the class. They were truly enjoying themselves. They were excited about every opportunity to try out a new piece of equipment—from an $11,000 Macintosh outfitted for video production, to a complex audiovisual system.

Only one of the hundreds of students who've been through the program has decided to major in computer science in college, but that doesn't bother Mr. Huber. Top Gun isn't about being a hotshot programmer. It's about learning how to use the tools that, as adults, these students will be exposed to and required to use at home and in the workplace. If his students can master these skills—and manage to have fun in the process—Mr. Huber has more than done his job.

Tools for the Times

In its 1995 report, *Growing Smart: What's Working for Girls in Schools,* the American Association of University Women identifies several steps teachers can take to ensure an equitable education for boys and girls. Among these: make learning about math and science fun; expect the same effort from girls and boys; and encourage students to work on projects and issues that have meaning for them.[20] Each of the three schools we've looked at in this chapter practices these principles every day in its classrooms and computer labs. In doing so they illustrate a powerful lesson: equity for girls doesn't mean forgetting about the boys or ignoring their interests. It's about creating an environment in which *all* students are given the opportunity and encouragement to succeed.

Lessons from Girls Schools

Once a year, boys at a school in Albany, New York, participated in a fun and educational activity: working with a local computer specialist, they'd roll up their sleeves, hunker down in a classroom for a day, and build two new computers from scratch. The students got hands-on experience assembling a computer, and the school received much-needed equipment in the bargain. It was a great project, except for one thing: no one asked the girls school to join in.

But in September 1995, the annual tradition got a much-needed facelift. This time, the students from neighboring Albany Academy for Girls got a turn. In just four hours, the group of seventh-grade girls—girls who had never assembled a computer before, girls who had little experience building *anything* before—built two new computers. They worked as a team, followed directions, and were done in half the time it took the boys to complete the same job.

"The instructor was amazed," recalls Susan Mumford, technology coordinator for the local girls school and herself the mother of two young women. "He'd never seen this kind of cooperation, the sense of sharing. It was terrific."

For the Girls

That little experiment speaks volumes about the power we all have to open up a new world of exploration for our daughters—a world that all too often is left for the boys. Throughout the country, girls schools such as this one are playing an integral role in providing girls and young women with hands-on computer experience. From New York to California, girls are assembling computers, creating multimedia presentations and sophisticated Web sites, and using the computer as a tool to facilitate research projects, assist in problem-solving, and develop high-level critical thinking skills.

The choice between a coed and a girls school is a complicated one, and the debate over which environment is best for our daughters is not going to be resolved in these pages. Whatever our thoughts about coed versus single-gender education, one thing is true: we can all learn a great deal about what works for girls educationally from the experiences of girls schools. Here, teachers can't avoid figuring out what appeals to girls. They can't ignore the girls who aren't interested in math, science, and computers. They must devise lesson plans that address girls' interests, coordinate activities that make technology real to them, and matriculate young women who are confident, capable, eager users of the tools of their times.

The following girls schools have done just that. They've struggled with the myriad issues facing all schools as they look for effective ways of using computers in and out of the classroom. They're still struggling with certain issues: developing a base level of competence and confidence among their teaching staffs, incorporating computer tools into a wide range of classes, and providing interested students with the encouragement and opportunity to pursue high-level computer courses.

Along the way, they are learning valuable lessons about what works for girls—and what doesn't.

Lesson Number 1:
Make Them Experts

About the same time those seventh-grade girls were assembling their first computers, their school was overhauling its technology plan. The goal: complete integration of computers and related technology across all disciplines, starting with the critical middle school years. In sixth, seventh and eighth grade, girls would learn to use a wide array of computer applications across all areas of study. They would become proficient in the use of a variety of hardware and software tools: from digital cameras and scanners, to multimedia presentation software, spreadsheets, and computer-based research. They would, in short, become experts in all the tools the school had to offer.

Why target middle school students? Because that's when girls begin to opt out of math and science and start to question the relevancy of these subjects to their lives. It is at this crucial time when the seeds of doubt are sown—doubts that have broad implications for years to come. There's no more critical time than middle-school years to expose girls to the many and varied uses of computers, to give them rich opportunities to explore their capabilities, and to lay a solid foundation that will give girls the skills and the confidence they need to explore other aspects of the technology during their high school years and beyond.

The cornerstone of their plan is "The Odyssey Project," a unique, interdisciplinary approach to technology integration that involves every sixth- and seventh-grade student. Working as a team, the faculty developed a series of six-week study units. Although each has a different area of emphasis—for example, one unit focuses on science, while another centers on a social studies topic—all of the units are designed to incorporate skills and activities across the subject areas. It is an ambitious project—and one that has changed forever the way students and teachers alike view the role of computers in the classroom.

The Odyssey Project officially began on November 6, 1996—the day after Bill Clinton was elected to his second term of office. The election that had captivated the attention of both students and teachers was an ideal subject to give the project a real-world flavor. Working in their social studies classes, students identified issues that the newly reelected president would face in the coming months and years. Among these: taxes, funding for the arts, welfare reform, free speech on the Internet, and immigration.

In their English classes, students then developed an opinion survey covering these topics and more, which they administered to friends and family over their Thanksgiving break. In math class the teachers wheeled in two carts holding eight Apple Powerbooks—notebook computers that traveled all over the school. Here seventh grader Georgia E. and her classmates got a quick refresher course in spreadsheets, then began entering their survey results, which they'd later graph and analyze. Although still a novice when it comes to spreadsheets, she was getting to be a pro at implementing the tool of choice for sharp-looking presentations: HyperStudio. "We're creating HyperStudio presentations in French, history, and in science. It's a great way to incorporate your own ideas into a presentation," she added.

Once all the data was in and accounted for, the students moved on to the next phase of the project: research. That was when the real fun—and learning—began. For the next three days, all regular classes were cancelled and every sixth- and seventh-grade girl was charged with just one task: research her topic, develop a position on the issue in question, then prepare a presentation, which the girls would deliver to their classmates and teachers in a town hall–type format. It was an ambitious project, to say the least, and one that had many skeptics at the school. Some thought giving the girls three days of unstructured time was asking for trouble. These were, after all, middle school girls. But the skeptics were proven wrong.

"I haven't seen any of the computer phobia people talk about among the girls. There's just a general excitement about computers," declares Robin Lyle, who teaches history to the middle school girls. She credits The Odyssey Project with generating that excitement. "With the laptops we now have the newest, fastest, smallest technology. There's a sense of fashion that comes into it all," she adds.

Over those three days, girls used all the resources the school had to offer—and then some. They commandeered the school's notebook computers and set up camp in the hallways or in out-of-the-way corners. They researched their topics on the Internet and used the school's CD-ROM encyclopedias. They called think tanks, government offices, and special interest groups. At one point Ms. Mumford got a confused call from the school secretary, who wasn't quite sure what to do with the onslaught of faxes pouring in to the school office— all of which were addressed to sixth- and seventh-grade girls.

When they had accumulated all the necessary information, the girls switched gears and began putting together their presentations. Many put their computer skills to work and created sophisticated multimedia presentations. Others took a decidedly low-tech approach and enacted skits to get their points across.

At the end of the three days the girls were exhausted. In their excitement about the project, many had barely stopped to take lunch breaks, let alone "fool around in the bathroom," as some of the skeptics on staff had predicted. In their critique of the project, students gave it rave reviews, but offered one suggestion: next time around, buy the students their own fax machine.

What made The Odyssey Project so successful? Planning played no small part in its success. The teachers met regularly to troubleshoot problems, discuss coordination issues, and revise the plan as needed. But all the planning in the world would not have yielded such phenomenal results had the students not played an integral role in the project. The girls—not the teachers—decided what issues to address, administered the surveys, figured out how best to research their topics, and selected the most effective format for presenting their information. They had a variety of tools at their disposal and were free to use any or all of them as they saw fit. And they used them all. Not because someone told them that creating a multimedia presentation would earn them a better grade, or because a teacher said it was important for them to learn how to conduct research on the Internet. They did it because they were passionate about the project, because they cared about the results.

The rest just came naturally.

Lesson Number 2:
Make It Mean Something

Compared with the complexities of designing projects for middle school girls, figuring out fun and educational ways to introduce second graders to computers might seem like a piece of cake. But while it is usually fairly easy to get eight-year-olds to sit in front of a computer, Judith Seidel, coordinator of computer instruction at The Brearley School on Manhattan's Upper East Side, wants to do more than that: "We want the girls to use the computer to create products that have meaning for them," she explains. That's why the beginning computer activities for second graders (computers aren't part of the curriculum for kindergartners or first graders) are agonized over, planned and planned again, and coordinated among the computer instructor and all the classroom teachers.

Although the girls spend some time playing educational games, the bulk of their computer time is spent on projects involving graphics and word-processing software. The activities are typically designed around a special school event, such as a parents' night, or a subject the students are studying in class. Each builds upon the next, so over the course of the year, students explore increasingly more complex features—and create increasingly sophisticated projects. Many of the activities involve designing and creating practical items that the girls or their families can actually use. This adds a personal dimension to the activities and also helps to reinforce the practical applicability of the tools they are learning to use.

Prior to Parents' Night, for example, the teachers used the school's digital camera to take photographs of each of the girls, who in turn incorporated those photos into labels of their own creation. Each label was a unique representation of its creator's interests and style. The labels served two purposes: the girls put them on their school belongings, and their parents used them as name tags on the big night.

Later in the year, as part of a unit on Africa, the girls designed their own stationery using Adinkra symbols from Ghana. Each of the sixteen designs symbolizes a different feeling or carries with it a different message ("Osram," for example, is shaped like a crescent moon and symbolizes female qualities of love and kindness; "Aya," the fern, represents defiance, independence, and fearlessness). The girls spent many class periods discussing the role of the symbols and their meaning in African cultures. To create their stationery, the girls each selected a few designs, which they used to create a pattern around the perimeter of the page. The product of their efforts was beautiful, original designs, which the girls gave to family and friends for the holidays.

Those second graders took away more from that project than just a couple of slips of writing paper, though. They also gained an appreciation for the capabilities of the software tools and for the value in learning how to use them. That's a lesson that will serve them well, long after the last piece of stationery has been used.

Lesson Number 3: Make It Fun

Many high-school girls would jump at the chance to surf the Web. But chatting and sending e-mail (two of the most popular online activities among teenagers) are not what most parents or teachers would describe as educational. What if you could take that fascination with the Web and use it to develop important skills—such as

Internet-based research techniques, and the ability to synthesize information from a variety of different sources? These would be valuable lessons, indeed. Well, teachers at St. Agnes Academy, a small, parochial high school for girls in the Southwest, have done just that.

Susan Boone, math teacher, faculty advisor for the school's computer club, and all-around computer evangelist, was the first teacher to design Internet-based lessons, creating a total of six different activities for students in her Algebra 1 class. But these aren't your typical math lessons. Although each of the assignments is designed to reinforce the concepts learned in class (linear equations, proportions, mean and median, and so on), they do so by exploring a variety of topics—some serious, some wacky.

In the lesson entitled, "A Functional Housing Market," for example, students use the Internet to research housing prices in their city and then calculate the cost per square foot of living space. In another lesson called "Pop Clock," students are asked to identify certain population and employment trends, using data from the Bureau of the Census Web page. Other choices are decidedly less serious: using the "Internet Pizza Server" (a site developed by a group of college students), students create their own pizza concoction and then use their order to calculate the area of different size pizzas and determine which size pizza is the better buy.

Although Boone was the first teacher to explore what

she calls "Netlearning," several of her associates have followed suit. Students in the senior literature class are using the Internet to research the internment of Japanese Americans during World War II. The economics class is playing a virtual stock market game on the Web, where they buy and sell stocks—and discover firsthand what a volatile market is all about. Sophomore biology students use the Internet to study chromosome mapping and the human genome project—all without ever leaving their PCs.

For many of the girls, these Internet-based lessons have been their first foray onto the World Wide Web. For others, they are a chance to explore new territory and hone their research skills, since each of the teachers encourages students to explore more than the few sites for which they've provided links. Several of the teachers also encourage students to go beyond presenting their information in a standard report format. Biology teacher Debbie Crank offered students extra credit points if they created a Web page on the chromosome they were responsible for researching. Fifteen students took her up on the offer. Most of the pages were just straightforward text screens with no fancy graphics—these girls, after all, had never taken a course in Web page design. But it was a start.

Without the lure of extra credit points, many of those girls would never have dreamed of trying to create a Web page. Now they know they can. Before the class assignments, many girls had never logged on to the Internet. Now they do—and not just to check e-mail. Like the girls in the other schools profiled in this chapter, these girls are learning how to use a variety of tools, but they're learning much more than that. They're learning the value of exploration, trying their hand at something new, going beyond just the basics. Along the way, they're discovering new interests and new talents. And there's no telling where those discoveries will take them.

9

50/50 by 2020

Fifty/fifty by 2020. Think of it as a mantra. Think of it as a call to action.

That's how Dr. Anita Borg, consulting engineer with Digital Equipment Corporation, thinks of it. Dr. Borg, a noted computer scientist and a tireless advocate for women in computer science, proposed the idea at a National Science Foundation (NSF) conference in December of 1995. The concept is quite simple: the scientific community must strive to produce an equal number of male and female graduates in science and engineering by the year 2020. It's a simple concept—but one that has profound consequences.

In the last quarter-century, women have made significant inroads in many fields once considered almost exclusively male territory. The number of female medical school graduates has risen from a paltry three percent in 1970 to thirty-eight percent in 1993, and nearly half of all law students are now women.[21] But computer science and engineering haven't benefited from these advances. Women remain a distinct minority, unable to gain full representation in these most exclusive of men's clubs.

The Numbers Game

In 1975, women received just under nineteen percent of all the bachelor's degrees awarded in computer science from PhD-granting universities. In 1976 the number went up slightly and continued to rise for the next ten years, reaching an all-time high of 37.2 percent in 1984. But then an alarming shift occurred. The numbers started to drop—first just a little (down to just under thirty-seven percent in 1985), and then a little more, and a little more, and a little more. By 1996 the number had plummeted to just sixteen percent—a twenty-year low at the very time when opportunities in the field were at an all-time high. The picture isn't much brighter when it comes to advanced degrees. Women earned twenty percent of all master's degrees in computer science in 1996, and just twelve percent of all PhDs in computer science and computer engineering.[22]

The shortage of women in computer science has been the source of articles in professional journals and speeches and presentations at professional conferences. The National Science Foundation (NSF) has published reports, major universities have established commissions to investigate the issue, and public and private organizations have organized a wide variety of programs—from summer sessions for high school girls to faculty mentors for undergraduate and graduate students—in an effort to increase the number of women in the field. But while there is anecdotal evidence that these programs help the individual participants tremendously, the net result has not been the kind of dramatic increases in degree production that many have hoped for. The vast majority of young women continue to make academic choices that steer them away from technology-related careers.

Critical Choices

Girls select out of science and engineering at a few critical points in their academic careers. The first occurs in high school, when girls—sometimes on the advice of a counselor, teacher, or parent—decide not to take the highest level math and science courses available to them. Although there is evidence to suggest that girls' participation in these courses is increasing, a higher percentage of boys than girls still take the highest level math and science courses. Boys also take more math and science in high school than girls. Seventy-one percent of the college-bound males in 1994 took four or more years of math, compared with sixty-eight percent of the college-bound females. The course-taking pattern is a little better in the sciences, with one notable exception: fifty-one percent of college-bound males in 1994 took physics in high school, compared to just forty-one percent of females.[23]

What accounts for the discrepancy? We know from research conducted by the AAUW that girls in high school are much more likely than boys to say they don't like math, they don't like science, and to doubt their abilities in both these areas. They're also more likely to question the relevancy of these high-level courses in their lives. Among high school students, for example, fifty-two percent of boys say they would enjoy being scientists, while only twenty-nine percent of girls believe science is a field they would enjoy.[24] If they don't think they're good at these subjects, and they don't plan on pursuing careers that require these skills, it's not hard to understand why girls would choose not to take these advanced classes.

It's at this point that adults should be doing everything possible to encourage young women to take advanced math and science courses. We should be offering assistance when they're struggling and praise when they're doing well. We should be helping them understand why higher-level math and science courses are important and the ramifications of opting out of these classes. And yet, research suggests that, in some instances, just the opposite may be happening. According to a 1994 NSF report, thirty-four percent of female high school students reported being advised not to take senior math, compared to twenty-six percent of male students. In science, thirty-two percent of female students reported being given such advice, compared with twenty-six percent of the male students.[25]

In many instances, teachers and counselors give this advice with the best of intentions. They've seen a young woman struggle through three years of high school math or science, and they think, *Why put her through a fourth year? She won't need the credits for college, anyway.* But that's exactly the wrong message to send to girls. Instead of helping them to opt out, we should be encouraging them to stay in.

Why? Because math is the gatekeeper, insists Dr. Danielle Bernstein, professor of computer science at Kean College in Union, New Jersey. Girls who don't take the highest-level courses available to them are effectively crossing many challenging—and lucrative—career choices off their list. It's not just that they enter college ill-prepared for the rigorous course work of a math or science major—they could, with support and determination make up for lost time during their freshman year. More importantly, a young woman who stops with just the required math or science courses typically doesn't see herself as technically proficient and therefore doesn't view a technical career as an option.

That's why Dr. Bernstein and her colleagues started Women into Science and Technology at Kean College, a program that introduces female high school students to careers in math, science, and technology through a career day for ninth graders, followed by ongoing newsletters and school visits by women scientists. "At the end of tenth grade girls are going to be asked if they're going to take math again. We want to grab them first so they have the right answer to that question," she explains.

Behind the Curve

Like advanced high school mathematics, high school programming courses are not a requirement for students interested in pursuing a computer science major. But they can make a world of difference in the comfort level of first-year students. Stacey Morrison, whose degree in computer science led her to a position at the Lyndon B. Johnson Space Center in Houston, discovered the hard way how important these earlier classes were. "I went to a small high school that really didn't offer programming courses," recalls Ms. Morrison. "Some of the people I was competing against had already studied Fortran or BASIC or maybe even Pascal in high school." Her professor didn't spend any time training students on how to run the compiler, or how to obtain a password, so Ms.

Morrison was left to muddle through on her own. "I kept getting Cs and I didn't know if I should keep up with it," she recalls, laughing as she remembers a friend telling her she could always sell computers if she didn't make it through the program. It's a bit funny to her now, but it wasn't funny then.

Ms. Morrison didn't have the option of taking programming in high school, but many young women make the choice not to take these courses. Although it is difficult to accurately measure female student enrollment in computer science courses, anecdotally, teachers report far fewer female than male students in these classes. One reason is that, like high-level mathematics courses, computer science (or programming) courses are generally electives—students aren't required to take the classes as a condition of graduation. As a result, students taking these courses are typically those who either enjoy programming, or who expect to pursue a university degree in a related field.

The clubby atmosphere in some advanced computer science courses may also contribute to the low representation of young women. Many of these classes are taught by teachers who love programming, and who delight in teaching students who share their passion. The environment can be quite stimulating for students who live to program, but it can also make for a threatening, unwelcome place for those who don't fit that mold.

A boys' club environment, however, is not the only way

to teach advanced computer science. Barbara Christopher has been teaching programming courses at her high school since 1984. Year after year, she continues to have as many girls in the class as boys. She doesn't sponsor any clubs or special programs for girls; she just teaches programming, not as a game, but as an extension of the critical thinking skills that will benefit young men and women alike.

"I have seen a lot of hacker-guru type teachers in computer science," says Mrs. Christopher. "They love programming for its own sake and feed off the excitement of teaching it to the students with real talent in the area. I like programming, but my aim is to give students logical thinking skills and programming just happens to be a fun way to develop them."

Although she teaches the honors course, Mrs. Christopher doesn't assume that students have had prior programming classes, and her teaching style tends to even out the different levels of experience among the students. "I teach in a step-by-step, logical way," she explains. "My tests cover exactly what I teach, and I have lots of small quizzes that prepare students for the major tests. My girls tend to have better study skills and my method of teaching rewards the organized, attentive student."

But in more ways than one, Mrs. Christopher is a rarity. Although women account for close to ninety percent of all early elementary (kindergarten through third grade) math and science teachers, their numbers dwindle as one progresses up through the grades. According to one survey, just over forty percent of the math teachers, and only thirty percent of the science teachers, for tenth through twelfth grade courses are women.

What Does a Woman Scientist Look Like?

It's not just a lack of preparation that keeps young women from pursuing careers in computer science. Interwoven with their lack of confidence and interest in technical fields is the absence of role models that young women can look to and aspire to be like. Put yourself in the position of a young woman in middle school or high school who's just beginning to think seriously about her career choices. She knows women who are teachers, writers, nurses, accountants, salespeople, and small business owners. She might even know women who are doctors and lawyers (or at least, she's seen women in these positions on TV). But how many girls know women who are engineers, mathematicians, or computer scientists? Not many.

For years, researchers have been conducting a simple, yet enlightening, experiment in which they ask school children to draw a picture of a scientist. Invariably, the image they draw is of a middle-aged white man wearing a lab coat and glasses. They don't draw a woman, and they don't draw a person of color.

Realizing that perceptions of scientists tend to be self-

fulfilling prophecies, some members of the scientific
community are stepping up efforts to increase the number of women in computer science and engineering and
focus on providing young women with role models in
these fields—women whom they can look up to and say,
"I want to be like her"; women who provide an alterna-
tive image.

One such effort is an attractive booklet developed by
the Computing Research Association's Committee on
the Status of Women in Computing Research (CRAW).
The booklet features eighteen women in computer science—from students to university professors to electrical
engineers and research scientists. Each of the profiles
provides a glimpse into the professional and the personal
lives of these accomplished women. There's Vicki Jones,
a research assistant in the department of computer science at the University of Illinois at Champaign-Urbana.
Dr. Jones spent four years working as a software engineer
in industry before deciding to return to school for her
PhD in computer science. Or Sandra Johnson Baylor, an
African American woman who is a computer engineer at
IBM's T. J. Watson Research Center. Baylor, who has her
PhD in electrical engineering, says she decided to pursue
an undergraduate degree in engineering after participating in a summer engineering institute on a university
campus. Or Susan Sim, an undergraduate student in
computer science, who started her academic career as an
art major, but switched to computer science when she

saw her boyfriend programming, and thought, *I can do this.*

It's an eclectic mix of women, each of whom defies the conventional image of a computer scientist. The booklet is given away to young women in high school and college, typically in conjunction with the presentation by a woman computer scientist. (One CRAW representative has even pulled together a sample presentation to accompany distribution of the booklet and made it available on the association's Web page.) The images and stories are reshaping the definition of who a scientist is—one woman at a time.

Picture Yourself on a College Campus . . .

Personal visits are critical, since they give girls an opportunity to meet and talk to a woman in computer science. They make the pictures and stories come alive and seem that much more real. Several universities have taken that interaction even further by creating summer programs (often with National Science Foundation backing) that link female high school and college students with female professors of computer science. The programs take many forms. Some are summer sessions during which high school girls have the opportunity to spend time on college campuses, and to live and work with both undergraduate computer science students and professors in the field while earning high school or college credit. Others are intense summer internships designed to give undergraduate women in computer science a taste of research life, working in conjunction with a female university professor.

The PipeLINK Project, which took place during the summer of 1995 at Rensselaer Polytechnic Institute (RPI) in Troy, New York, brought together three generations of women and girls: a small group of undergraduate computer science majors spent the summer at RPI working on research projects with female professors in science and engineering. Then, during the last two weeks of their internship, the students served as mentors for high school girls, who were treated to total immersion into life on a college campus. They took courses in e-mail, Web design, robotics, and programming. They listened to undergraduate and graduate students talk about what it's like to major in computer science. They toured laboratories and talked with the older women about careers in the field.

PipeLINK was the brainchild of Dr. Ellen Walker and her colleague, Dr. Susan Rodger. "It grew out of a discussion we were having about our own experiences," recalls Walker. "We asked ourselves what would have been good for us when we were in high school." The answer to the women was obvious: role models and mentors. "As it turns out there are a lot of women in computer science, but I never knew about them in high school," says Dr. Walker. "And when you don't know about them, the stereotype of a nerdy guy with stringy hair and no social skills takes hold instead. That's an image that turns girls off, particularly in middle school and high school when they're concerned about being social."

Jyotsna Advani read about PipeLINK on the World Wide Web when she was a junior computer science major at Bryn Mawr, and was excited about the opportunity to work on a research project with a university professor. "I got assigned to work with a professor in mechanical engineering and initially I was disappointed that it wasn't in computer science. But I ended up really enjoying it," says the native of India. And what about the mentoring part of the program? "It was nice to be able to communicate all my ideas. I get a tremendous amount of satisfaction when I can see the light in the person's face," she adds. Jyotsna is now a first-year graduate student in computer science. Did PipeLINK convince her to pursue an advanced degree? "Well, I was of two minds about what I wanted to do after graduation, and the experience with the program helped reinforce my confidence in doing research and working independently in the field of computer science." In other words, the program worked; it achieved exactly what Dr. Walker had hoped it would.

Many institutions have similar programs, all based on the concept that the more girls can get to know women who've pursued careers in computer science, the more they will consider the field as an option for themselves. Although there is no replacement for face-to-face contact, several groups are also taking advantage of girls' interest in e-mail to start what's been termed telementoring—where one or more female high school or college students are partnered with a woman in the field.

Dr. Anne Tyrie is a telementor. She and her mentee, a high school student in Texas, exchange e-mail at least once a week. Although Dr. Tyrie shares with her mentee the ins and outs of her life as a computer scientist, she doesn't stress the technical part of the job. "Nearly every e-mail, I tell her what I'm currently doing and point out to her that although I am heavily involved in information technology, most of what I do is people-oriented. In telling her what I do day to day, none of which talks about CP 3000s or what have you, she'll be absorbing that my job is about relationship-building and people skills. I'm hoping that's the case, anyway."

Like many of the participating high school students, Dr. Tyrie's mentee rarely asks questions about computer science or other technical subjects. Her e-mail messages are usually about what's going on at home or at school, or the latest happenings with her boyfriend. At first, many of the mentors were concerned—and perhaps a little disappointed—at the nature of the dialogue. This was, after all, their opportunity to share their expertise. They hadn't planned on talking about boy problems. But Dr. Tyrie is now philosophical about the dialogue. "We're supporting one another, and that's what mentoring is all about. It's not necessarily about discussing specific issues." She does, however, try to take advantage of every opportunity to affect, even in subtle ways, the way her student views herself and her options after college. When her mentee says she's waiting for her boyfriend to call, for example, Dr. Tyrie will suggest she go ahead and call him if she wants to talk. She's also learned to be more aware of underlying issues behind what the student she's corresponding with may be writing. "A seventeen-year-old doesn't say I have poor self-image. It just comes through in what she's talking about. I have to be aware of this and respond to those issues in a very supportive and humorous way."

Whether online or in person, these mentoring programs are invaluable—both for the student and the teacher. However, they are only the first step. As important as these programs are, it's not enough to simply encourage girls to pursue careers in nontraditional fields. We also need to recognize the unique set of issues facing the young women who choose this less-traveled path.

Life as a Female CS Major

Encouraging young women to consider computer science is one thing. Providing an environment in which they can thrive and excel is quite another. When they enter computer science programs, young women are faced with isolation and loneliness, hostility and sexism. They must make it through four years of rigorous course work while at the same time trying to cope with the pressures associated with being one of a few women among many men.

A recent study by a committee chartered by the Massachusetts Institute of Technology's Department of Electrical Engineering and Computer Science to investigate the disparity in male/female undergraduate enrollment vividly illustrates some of the issues facing female computer science and engineering majors. Although the committee's findings are based solely on MIT students, they do offer important insight into the general undergraduate experience of female computer science majors.

As part of its research, the MIT committee conducted two surveys of its undergraduates. The first consisted of a series of questions addressed to two groups of women: thirty-two women who had indicated an interest in computer science or electrical engineering on their application for admission, but who had ultimately chosen other majors, and twenty-eight women who had not indicated an interest in either field on their application, yet had wound up majoring in one of the two areas nonetheless. The second survey was administered to all men and women in core computer science or electrical engineering courses.

Although the committee found many similarities among all the groups surveyed, it also uncovered some important differences, particularly in the areas of preparation for the major and confidence in one's abilities—

two factors critical to a successful undergraduate career in these demanding fields.

"The most notable result," according to the committee's final report, "is that women, much more so than men, feel that they have come to MIT 'less prepared to major in electrical engineering and computer science' than their peers." Among the EECS majors surveyed during the fall of 1994, thirty-five percent of the men felt they were less prepared than their classmates; sixty-five percent of the women felt that way according to the report. At least one female student who rated her background as below average had taken the computer science advanced placement exam. (These exams are typically taken by students who've taken advanced-level courses in the subject during high school.)[26]

Not surprisingly, men and women alike viewed the course as very competitive, but women's answers to one of the questions indicates just how competitive the environment is. When asked if they thought the course was too competitive, women were largely neutral in their responses. When asked whether other women in the program found the course too competitive, most women answered yes.

Could it be that the women didn't dare admit their insecurities? It was much safer, judging from the responses, for a woman to attribute those feelings to one of her classmates than to personally acknowledge even the slightest bit of insecurity about the coursework, however rigorous. Regardless of where they attended school, in interview after interview, women I spoke with addressed the fiercely competitive nature of computer science programs—the seemingly endless battle to finish first, get the highest score, and to never let on that you're struggling.

"I haven't found anyone to bond with," says eighteen-year-old Cindy N., a freshman computer science major at the University of Arizona, where the ratio of men to women in the CS department is about ten to one. "It's been hard and I have this insecurity of thinking I'm the only one in that boat." Cindy recalls one of the first classes she took in which there were about 180 men and only six women. "It was *sooo* hard and the other people in the class always seemed to understand everything," she recalls, groaning as she remembers the experience. She went to the professor for help, but he only succeeded in making her feel even less prepared. She asked classmates how they were doing, but none of them seemed to need any help. "Unfortunately I decided to drop the course halfway through because I was only getting a sixty percent. In the end, the grading scale was adjusted so that seventy percent was an A." It wasn't that Cindy didn't have the "chops" to make it as a computer science major. She just didn't have the confidence of some of her male peers.

Cindy learned from that experience and now starts

study groups at the beginning of each class. When necessary, she seeks out the help of teaching assistants and professors to clarify material before a test. Her proactive approach has helped, she says, but life as a female computer science major is never easy.

When You're Not One of the Guys

Emily R. is at the opposite end of her college career from Cindy. She's a senior computer science major who has managed to beat the odds and complete the rigorous work—but it hasn't been easy. "In some of my classes, I get the impression guys have been playing with computers and video games their whole life," says the twenty-two-year-old senior. "The guys will sleep through class and have an attitude like it's all old hat." In contrast, she observes, the women take every lecture, every assignment intensely seriously. "Even one girl who never has scored less than ninety-five on any test says she would never think of skipping class or turning something in late for fear she'd be hopelessly behind."

It's not that Emily and her female classmates know any less than their male counterparts. When you're one of a very small minority, the entire environment—let alone the rigorous classes—can make you question your abilities, question why you're there. The insecurities that cause a young high school woman to doubt her abilities in math and science don't miraculously fall by the wayside when she enters college. Often they're still there, dogging her with each assignment.

"More than people judging me, I judged myself all along," Emily confesses. "I never felt like I really fit in to the department. I never felt like I was a computer scientist. Even the woman who is the hotshot in the department said that at times she felt she didn't fit in."

Women who earned their degrees in the 1970s and 1980s tell stories about working in labs where there were *Playboy* calendars on computers and classmates frequently made blatantly sexist remarks. In some instances, the culture has improved, but not a lot. The lab environment in particular—where computer science majors live for their first few years—is not a friendly place for women.

"Even doing my homework was difficult," says twenty-six-year-old Rachel Rubin, who received her undergraduate degree in computer science from Carnegie Mellon University in Pittsburgh. "I'd walk into the computer science cluster where there were rows and rows of workstations. I'd try to just sit down and do my thing, but everyone would turn and look at me." There was one male student who would send her e-mail the minute she sat down, telling her how good-looking she was and asking if she wanted to talk. "It freaked me out," she says.

Rachel made it through, she says, because she was determined not to fail. She has one regret: that she didn't develop a support group to sustain her through the rough times.

Finding Strength in Numbers

Unlike Rachel, Emily made certain that she found that help. During her junior year she organized an informal support group, consisting of three female computer science majors (there were only six in the entire program) and two female chemistry majors. They'd meet regularly to talk, share stories, and give one another support and encouragement. She also joined the local chapter of Webgrrls, a national organization for women working in Web-related fields, and subscribed to a variety of online mailing lists for women in technical fields. Each of these activities helped her to feel a little less alone, a little more connected with a community of women with like interests and like concerns.

On university campuses throughout the country, women in computer science and engineering have formed associations—some formal, some casual. They host faculty-student gatherings, organize study groups, pair first- and second-year undergraduates with third- and fourth-year students, and offer female students a community of support and encouragement that they often cannot find elsewhere. For many young women, this support structure is as critical to their academic success as their technical skills.

Dr. Anita Borg (of 50/50 fame) knows the importance of community and establishing mentoring relationships. In 1987, she started Systers, an electronic community for technical women in computing. Today, Systers has 2500 members in twenty-five countries, and provides an international community of advice and support. Although it started as a professional organization, it now also includes women pursuing undergraduate and graduate degrees in computer science.

Cindy, the freshman computer science major, can attest to the value of the list. In the summer between her senior year in high school and her freshman year in college, she was hired for a position with an Internet provider, only to be harassed by the male applicant whom she beat out for the job. "He sent me e-mail saying the reason I was hired first wasn't because I had more qualifications, but because I'm female. He implied that I'd slept with the boss or something." Cindy wasn't sure what to do, so she posted a message about the experience to the Systers mailing list. In one day she received 300 e-mail messages from women offering their advice, support, and encouragement.

"I cooled down a bit and then sent the guy e-mail telling him how I felt about his message. Later he came back and apologized," says Cindy.

Although the Systers mailing list has at times been criticized for not allowing men to join, Dr. Borg holds fast to her belief that maintaining communities that are

women-only is vital in an environment so overwhelm-
ingly dominated by men.

In a 1993 article entitled, "Why Systers?" she wrote,
"Systers is not analogous to a private all-male club. It is
different because women in computer science are a small
minority of the community. . . . I have not addressed
whether a forum such as Systers would be necessary in
an ideal and egalitarian world. . . . When we get there,
we can make that decision."

Every woman I spoke with in this field stressed their
need for some form of support and encouragement. For
some women, their parents—and perhaps later, a partner—provided that support. For many others, the association with women in similar circumstances was critical.
It provided them a place to share experiences such as
Cindy's, a place they could go to ask for help and advice,
and a place to make friends. Some women also joined
coed societies, but in college and later in their professional lives these female-only groups have provided a
level of encouragement and support unmatched, even
by the best coed group.

When I spoke to Emily she had already made it through
the academics and was starting to consider job opportunities. Cindy, though only a freshman, was eagerly tackling her major. Many women don't get that far, though.
The competitive atmosphere, the isolation (besides the
small number of female students, there are also very few
women faculty members to look to as mentors), and the

macho nature of some of the programs make for a higher attrition rate among female computer science and engineering students than among their male counterparts.

Jennifer H. is one of those statistics. A twenty-one-year-old junior, she entered college as a computer science major, but wound up switching to business after the first year. Throughout high school, Jennifer liked math, science, and computers. She was good at these areas, too. But after her first computer science course—an honors course—at her university, she swore she would never take another class in the department again. Yet it wasn't the work she had trouble with. Jennifer got an A in the class. It was the competitive, macho atmosphere that she wanted no part of.

"It's like death by a thousand cuts," elaborates one woman I spoke with. "It's a lot of little things that all add up to something large. The little comments and the attitudes you encounter may not seem like large things, but the fact is that women and minorities deal with these experiences on a daily basis. It all just accumulates."

Looking Toward 2020

Why should we care if Emily or Jennifer or Cindy make it through four years as an undergraduate computer science major? Why does it matter if talented young women

choose careers outside computer science and engineering?

Because they are our future.

According to the U.S. Department of Labor, computer scientists and systems analysts will account for two
of the five fastest growing job categories between now
and the year 2005. The computer industry offers some
of the best-paying, most leading-edge jobs available.
Right now, the majority of those high-paying, fast-track
jobs go to men. But the trend can't continue. America
faces a shortfall in scientists and engineers by the year
2005, and that shortfall is expected to hit at the same
time that women will account for nearly fifty percent of
the U.S. labor force. Allowing talented young women to
choose other paths is a folly we can no longer afford.

Encouraging young women to pursue careers in
computer science and engineering isn't just about economics. We need women in these positions because they
bring something different to the equation than men. We
need a diversified pool of talent creating the tools that
men and women, boys and girls, will be using well into
the twenty-first century.

And we should want and expect as much for our
daughters as we do for our sons.

10

Bridging the Gap

Strategies for Change

Raising awareness about the inequalities surrounding girls and computers is an important first step, but it's only a first step. It's not enough to simply acknowledge the inequities that pervade all aspects of computing—we need to actively work on changing them. Parents, teachers, school counselors, and other caring adults all have a role to play in this process. It's hard to imagine why anyone would intentionally tell a young girl that computer skills are unimportant, that boys are better at computers than girls, or that we shouldn't care that the vast majority of computer scientists and engineers are men. And yet, in a very real sense, that's what our actions—and our inactions—say to our daughters every day.

What follows are straightforward, practical ways in which we can work to shape a new image of computing for our daughters—at home, at school, and, as they get older, at work. It's time to introduce our daughters to a world in which girls are active, eager computer users. A world where girls play games, surf the Web, tinker with hardware, and create new software programs. A world where being into computers doesn't mean being a geek or a nerd. A world where girls can explore, excel, and be active participants in the discoveries that are changing the way each of us works and plays.[27]

Encouragement@Home

The first place to start shaping our daughters' computer fitness is at home. It's here where initial patterns of behavior are set and here where girls first begin to understand their true potential.

Be aware of inequitable patterns of computer use. Consider setting up the computer in a room that's easily accessible to the entire family, such as a family room, kitchen, or spare bedroom. Avoid putting it in one child's room. Make the computer area as inviting and friendly as possible.

Make sure that computer time is distributed equitably among all the family members. If necessary, establish a schedule that guarantees everyone time at the keyboard. Give schoolwork the top priority, followed by fun time for everyone. Hint: If you approach computer time as a privilege, teenage girls are more likely to look forward to their turn at the mouse.

Encourage exploration. Don't insist upon guiding your daughter through a new computer game or a new software tool. Let her explore it on her own. If it's a well-designed program (and many aren't, so choose carefully), a child in the suggested age range should be able to navigate through its features or activities on her own. You'll want to stay close by—to answer questions and to familiarize yourself with the program. Just make sure your daughter's in the driver's seat.

Involve your daughter in software purchases. Once you've read software reviews and narrowed your choices down to a few selections, discuss the purchase with your daughter. Take her with you to the store; show her the programs you're considering and describe each one to her. (Some stores even have computers set up where customers can try out software themselves before making the final purchase.) Look for programs that have male and female characters in the lead, and programs that offer a variety of different activities or points of entry—such as an exploration mode, as well as a question-and-answer mode.

After you've explored all the options, let your daughter make the final selection. She will get more than just a new computer program from these shopping expeditions—she'll learn early on that the computer store isn't just a place where guys hang out. As your daughter gets older, encourage her to do her own research and to suggest to you games she's interested in trying out.

Be familiar with the computer games your children play. Dr. Patrick O'Heffernan, chairman of the Children's Information Trust, suggests parents learn how to play the games their children are playing. "Don't stop at the first or second level," he advises, noting that often the most violent or sexually explicit scenes don't appear until players have progressed to some of the highest levels in a game.

If you object to violent games or games that depict women as victims or sex objects, talk to your children about why this software is off limits and help to find fun, challenging alternatives. The limitations don't have to be viewed as some type of punishment, provided you explain your reservations honestly and clearly with your children. If you're talking to your son (most girls aren't interested in these games), ask him how he would feel to have his mother, sister, or a close girlfriend treated in the same way women are treated in many of the popular games. Offer suggestions as to how he can gracefully decline playing the games at a friend's house.

Be a positive role model. It's especially important that daughters see their mothers using the computer—for work *and* for fun. Don't always wait until the kids are in bed before playing a game, checking your stocks, or balancing your checkbook.

Ask your daughter for help. Take advantage of your daughter's expertise. Ask her to show you how to set up an e-mail account, or how to search for a topic on the Internet. The more questions you ask her, the more you'll learn—and the better she'll feel about herself and her abilities.

Look for activities you and your daughter can do together. Some schools or local organizations, such as the American Association of University Women (AAUW), sponsor mother-daughter computer days. This is a great opportunity to spend a day exploring computers with your daughter.

Take your daughter to work. When appropriate, show your daughter how you use your computer at your job. When feasible, bring her to the office on weekends. Let her type a letter to a friend, work on a paper for school, play a game of computer solitaire, or send e-mail to a friend.

Introduce your daughter to technical women. Parents can introduce their daughters to female friends or relatives who have jobs in computer-related fields. Encourage these women to discuss the fun, as well as the practical side, of their career choice. What do they find the most exciting or challenging aspect of their profession? Do they travel? Have they met interesting people? Have they been associated with any of the products your daughter may have used? What courses in school were most helpful in preparing for their career?

Take advantage of resources in your community. Many libraries now have computers available to the public. Investigate summer programs through the local recreation and parks department, school district, or private camps or learning centers. (Many of these programs offer scholarships for needy students.)

Plan a trip to the museum. Many cities are now home to science, technology, and discovery museums, many of which have hands-on activities and exhibits designed for children and teens. These centers can make terrific outings, either for a family or a class. Keep in mind, though, that a trip to a computer museum with her parents may not be an older girl's first choice for a Saturday afternoon activity, so parents with teenage girls should consider encouraging their daughter to invite a friend or two along.

Attend an Expanding Your Horizons conference. Middle school and high school girls can benefit tremendously from participation in these day-long events (typically held in March in cities throughout the United

States). The events are usually held on college campuses and include a variety of workshops where girls get to participate in hands-on science and math activities. There are also workshops designed specifically for parents and teachers, offering strategies for encouraging girls to explore nontraditional fields.

Look for fun, "cool" computer activities that adolescent girls will enjoy. Introduce them to some of the new software designed just for them. Take them to a meeting of Webgrrls, a national organization for women whose jobs involve the World Wide Web.

Encourage your daughter in her efforts. All girls, regardless of their abilities, need to be complimented and encouraged. Tell your daughter you're proud of her. Compliment her on her work. Buy her a book on how to design Web pages—then suggest that she create a page for your family. Clip out articles about new sites or new software programs that you think will be of interest.

Spend time exploring the Web with your daughter. Help her to locate sites devoted to subjects or hobbies she's interested in. Show her some of the many sites by and for preteen and teenage girls.

Set up an e-mail account and investigate chat areas. Make sure that you establish clear guidelines for online use. Discuss which sites are acceptable and which are not. Educate your children about the potential dangers online. Make sure they know never to provide anyone with their name, phone number, or the city in which they live. Explain that they always have an out—they can log off if they're ever made to feel uncomfortable by someone else's online behavior. Be sure to address this topic carefully. You want them to be safe and aware, but you don't want to scare them off potentially rewarding explorations.

Encouragement@School

Besides challenging and encouraging our daughters at home, we need to make sure that they're given every opportunity to explore and excel at school. Parents, teachers, counselors, and school administrators all have a role to play in this effort.

Encourage girls to take the highest level math and science courses available to them in school. These courses help students to develop the critical-thinking and problem-solving skills that are vital to many professions—not just careers in computer science or engineering. Don't wait for female students to sign up for these classes. Counselors, teachers, and parents should all encourage them to do so.

When necessary, provide girls with extra help in advanced math or science classes. Parents and teachers should strategize on ways to help girls improve their abilities, and bolster their confidence in these critical areas. If possible, arrange for a private tutor or start an after-school tutoring session. Remember: girls will often view anything less than an A as failure. Take every opportunity to congratulate a girl on her successes and to remind her how smart she is.

Find out about the computer activities at your daughter's school. Is there a computer club? Do girls participate? If after-hours computer activities are dominated by boys, meet with the advisor to discuss ways to attract more girls. Encourage the school to consider forming a girls' computer or technology club—and then volunteer to help out. Be careful, though, not to schedule any after-school computer activities at the same time as other popular extracurricular clubs or activities.

Investigate the type of educational software available at your daughter's school. Talk to the computer instructor about stocking a variety of educational software programs—programs with girls, as well as boys, as the lead character, programs that offer users a variety of different ways to play, such as an exploration mode, as well as a timed or point-driven activity.

Be on the lookout for inequities in the classroom.
Teachers need to be aware of the many ways in which
their teaching style can help to determine a girl's success
or failure in class. Take care to call on boys and girls
equally. Resist the urge to show girls how to solve a problem
or how to use a specific computer function. Encourage
girls to discover the answers for themselves through
trial and error.

Make sure all students benefit from computer use.
In many classrooms, the computer is one of many activities
available to students after they've finished the
required work. Teachers should be careful that a few
students aren't allowed to monopolize the computer. Consider
establishing a schedule that gives each child the
opportunity to use the computer at least once a week.

**Be careful to plan lessons that appeal to girls and
boys equally.** Look for ways to incorporate art, sports,
or music themes into a computer lesson. Don't expect
students to be inherently interested in learning how to
recalculate a spreadsheet. Make the lesson fun and applicable
to their daily lives.

Design collaborative activities. Group projects can
be an effective way of getting girls excited and interested
in math and science. Select the groups carefully, though,

so that the more experienced computer users don't dominate an activity.

Exploit the Web. Capitalize on girls' interest in the Web by creating an Internet-based lesson. Post the assignment on the Web and then encourage students to use search engines to research relevant sites.

Promote girls as experts. Too often, teachers defer to boys as the computer experts in class. Teachers should seek out opportunities to have older, more experienced girls serve as mentors for younger students. This can be a tremendous way of boosting a girl's self-esteem and encouraging everyone—students and teachers alike—to view her as the expert that she is.

Emphasize the importance of computer skills. Make sure girls recognize the critical role computer skills play in a variety of careers and professions—from graphic artists to clothing designers, from accountants to architects. Teachers can invite women of different professions to their classes and have them discuss how they use computers in their work.

Highlight the accomplishments of women. The media is full of pictures and stories about men and their contributions to the field of computing, but many girls have never heard of Lady Ada Byron, the first computer programmer, or Admiral Grace Hopper, the creator of the first compiler and the "mother" of COBOL. There are several excellent resources on women in computer science on the World Wide Web, complete with pictures and biographies of notable women.

Expect the Best

Too often, our society expects less of girls than we do of boys. We expect boys to be able to run faster and jump higher; we expect them to be better at math, better at science, to be better at—and more interested in—computers.

Our daughters sense that we expect something different from them—*something less from them*—than we do from our sons. They get that message when no one stops a boy as he tries to grab the mouse out of a girl's hand. They take note of how frequently a teacher calls on a boy to demonstrate a computer activity, when the girls in class know it just as well. And they definitely are affected every time they see a woman bewildered by computers—or hear a man or boy act as though she should be.

Some girls are able to get beyond these messages. With the help and encouragement of a teacher or parent they've been able to discover the many capabilities computers have to offer, and to develop their own talents in this critical area. They've started online computer clubs, created sophisticated Web sites, participated in award-winning programming or research activities. They won't all become computer scientists or electrical engineers, but some will. Others may design Web pages or use their computer skills to start their own graphics or marketing business.

Whether our daughters become software developers or school teachers, nurses or nuclear physicists, computers are guaranteed to be an integral part of their adult lives. They'll use computers to communicate with friends, relatives, and business associates. They'll use computers to plan vacations, shop for goods and services, balance their checkbooks, perhaps one day even to vote.

It's our job to make sure our daughters have the skills they'll need to be productive workers and active members of their communities. We must teach our daughters that computers are fun, exciting, incredibly powerful tools that can help them to be more creative, more productive individuals.

It's up to us to create an environment in which every girl has the opportunity to learn, to explore, to excel. Only then will Jane—and all her sisters—know that her interest in computers is real, valuable, and that she does, indeed, compute.

Resources

The following lists are just a sampling of the many computing resources for girls. Use them as a starting point, and then begin exploring on your own—and encourage the young girl in your life to do the same. You'll be amazed at what you'll find.

Online Sites

The World Wide Web is an ever-changing place and new sites are added daily. For help locating interesting Web sites, run a search using one of the many Web search tools, such as Yahoo (http://www.yahoo.com), or Femina (http://www.femina.com), a search tool that specializes in cataloging sites for women and girls. Just type in the subject you're interested in (such as "horses" or "soccer,") and the search tool will do the rest. Another great resource for preteen and teenage girls interested in learning more about the Web is *Tech Girl's Internet Ad-*

ventures, by Girl Tech (IDG Books Worldwide, Foster City, 1997). The book includes software that enables girls to create their own Web sites, as well as descriptions of more than a hundred fun and educational sites.

Club Girl Tech

http://www.girltech.com

Online games, chats, and message boards for girls, along with research on girls and computers that parents and teachers will find interesting.

Cybergrrl

http://www.cybergrrl.com

This Web site includes links to the Femina search tool, as well as Webgrrls, a national organization for women in Web-related businesses. Many local Webgrrls chapters sponsor events for preteen and teenage girls.

FreeZone

http://www.freezone.com

A fun coed site that includes a variety of activities just for girls, including girls chat nights and girls message board areas.

Girls Interwire Planet Girl

http://www.girlgamesinc.com/

A site for pre-teen and teenage girls from the developers of *Let's Talk About Me,* a computer game for girls.

Horse Country Online

http://www.horse-country.com/

The ultimate horse site, written and produced primarily by women and girls.

NewMoon

http://www.newmoon.org

The online version of the popular magazine written by, for, and about girls.

Women of NASA

http://quest.arc.nasa.gov/women

An excellent resource designed to encourage girls in math and science by providing real-world examples of women in these fields.

WomenSpace

http://www.womenspace.com

Despite the name, this site includes a messaging area where girls can post their thoughts on serious subjects, such as depression, or add their own stories to the "Totally Embarrassing Tales" area.

Girl-Friendly Software

Here's a sampling of some top-rated software for girls of all ages. Two guides to new software include: *Newsweek's Parent's Guide to Children's Software '97*, and *That's Edu-*

tainment! By Eric Brown (Osborne McGraw Hill, Berkeley, 1995). On the Web, Children's Software Revue (http://www.microweb.com/pepsite/Revue/revue.html) offers excellent reviews of the latest children's software. A printed newsletter is also available bimonthly.

Ages 3-6

The House Series
http://www.edmark.com

Highly rated early reading, math, and science programs that feature a variety of activities for preschoolers.

Edmark
6727 185th Ave., NE
Redmond, WA 98073-3218
800-426-0856

The Living Books Series
http://www.broderbund.com

Interactive storybooks for preschoolers with plenty of "clickables" to encourage exploration.

Living Books
800-776-4724

PlaySkool Puzzles
http://www.hasbro.com

Children can make their own jigsaw puzzles using drawing and coloring tools, or solve one of the dozens that're included in the game.

Hasbro Interactive
50 Dunham Rd.
Beverly, MA 01915
800-638-6927

The Putt Putt and Freddi Fish Series

http://www.humongous.com

Interactive scavenger hunts that feature beautiful animation, hidden objects, and wonderful characters for
children as old as eight to explore.

Humongous Entertainment
16932 Woodinville-Redmond Rd., NE, Suite 204
Woodinville, WA 98072
800-499-8386

Ages 6-8

Barbie Fashion Designer

http://www.mattelmedia.com

Although Barbie isn't every parent's choice of role models for their young daughter, this is a uniquely creative
software program for designing and creating Barbie
clothes and accessories.

Mattel Media
333 Continental Boulevard
El Segundo, CA 90245
888-628-8359

Kid Pix Studio

http://www.broderbund.com

This classic art program has all the tools younger computer artists need, including drawing tools, stamps, and more.

Broderbund Software
P.O. Box 6125
Novato, CA 94948-6125
800-521-6263

The Madeline Series

http://www.creativewonders.com

A fun and educational series of games based on the popular storybook character.

Creative Wonders
595 Penobscot Drive
Redwood City, CA 94063
800-543-9778

The Magic School Bus Series

http://www.microsoft.com

These exploration CD-ROMs based on the popular Scholastic series include titles on the solar system, dinosaurs, and the ocean.

Microsoft Corporation
One Microsoft Way
Redmond, WA 98052
800-426-9400

PrintPaks Multimedia Crafts

http://www.printpaks.com

Innovative creativity packs for making everything from magnets to jewelry on your computer. They're easy enough for young children to use, but fun enough for the whole family to enjoy.

PrintPaks
513 NW 13th Avenue, Suite 209
Portland, OR 97209
800-774-6860

Ages 9-12

American Girls Premier

http://www.learningco.com

Working with The Pleasant Company, this long-time leader in educational software is releasing a creativity program based on the American Girls story collection.

The Learning Company
One Athenauem St.
Cambridge, MA 02142
800-227-5609

The Babysitters Club Clubhouse Activity Center

http://www.creativewonders.com

An interactive journal, organizer, and creativity kit based on characters from the popular book series.

Creative Wonders
595 Penobscot Drive
Redwood City, CA 94063
800-543-9778

The Carmen Sandiego Series

http://www.broderbund.com

An excellent mystery series in which players test their knowledge of geography and hone their problem-solving skills.

> Broderbund Software
> P.O. Box 6125
> Novato, CA 94948-6125
> 800-521-6263

Hollywood High

http://www.theatrix.com

Players write, direct and produce their own animated stories.

> Theatrix Interactive
> 1250 45th Street
> Emeryville, CA 94608-2924
> 800-955-8749

Let's Talk About Me! Some More

http://www.girlgamesinc.com

Dubbed an "interactive handbook" for preteen and teenage girls, this new genre of game includes a number of different activities, including a diary, quizzes, and profiles of accomplished women.

> Davidson/Simon & Shuster Interactive
> 19840 Pioneer Ave.
> Torrance, CA 90503
> 800-457-8357

The Oregon Trail

http://www.learningco.com

The multimedia game that brings the pioneers' trek across the Oregon Trail to life.

> The Learning Company
> One Athenauem St.
> Cambridge, MA 02142
> 800-227-5609

Rockett's New School,
Secret Paths in the Forest

http://www.purple-moon.com

Two new friendship adventures for preteen girls.

> Purple Moon
> 1091 Shoreline Blvd.
> Mountain View, CA 94043
> 888-278-7753

13 and Older

Myst

http://www.broderbund.com

A surrealistic adventure game that captivated the attention of many women and older girls.

> Broderbund Software
> P.O. Box 6125
> Novato, CA 94948-6125
> 800-521-6263

Microsoft Publisher

http://www.microsoft.com

A sophisticated but easy-to-use desktop publishing package for creating cards, calendars, and more.

Microsoft Corporation
One Microsoft Way
Redmond, WA 98052
800-426-9400

Company to Watch

Girl Tech

http://www.girltech.com

This start-up company is developing games and hi-tech toys for preteen girls.

Girl Tech
851 Irwin St., Suite 100
San Rafael, CA 94901
415-256-1510

Helpful Organizations

The following organizations offer a variety of programs and resources for young girls, as well as for parents and teachers interested in developmental and equity issues.

American Association of University Women

http://www.aauw.org/

1111 Sixteenth St., N.W.
Washington, D.C. 20036
202-785-7700

The AAUW has funded several ground-breaking studies on issues facing girls. Local branches sponsor a variety of programs designed to encourage girls in nontraditional areas, including math, science, and computers.

Expanding Your Horizons Math/Science Network
http://www.elstad.com/msneyh.html

e-mail: msneyh@ella.mills.edu
Mills College
5000 MacArthur Blvd.
Oakland, CA 94613
510-430-2222

Expanding Your Horizons conferences for middle school and high school girls are held in cities throughout the country. These day-long events are typically held on a university campus and are designed to expose girls to a wide variety of careers and interests in math, science, and technology-related fields.

Girls, Incorporated
http://www.girlsinc.org

30 East 33rd Street
New York, NY 10016-5394
212-689-3700

Local affiliates sponsor numerous programs for girls, including Eureka and Operation SMART, designed to encourage girls in math, science, technology, and other nontraditional areas.

Girl Scouts of the USA
http://www.girlscouts.org

> 420 Fifth Avenue
> New York, NY 10018
> 212-852-8000

Local councils are creating Web pages, opening up computer centers, and sponsoring summer computer camps for girls. At a national level, Girl Scouts is revamping its recognitions to incorporate expanded use of computer technology.

GirlTECH
Center for Research in Parallel Computation
http://www.crpc.rice.edu/CRPC/Women/GirlTECH

GirlTECH sponsors a summer program in which teachers receive intensive technology training and explore teaching strategies that impact gender equity in the classroom. The Web site includes information on gender equity issues in math, science, and computing.

Computer Camps and Programs

It should come as no surprise that computer camps are using the World Wide Web to advertise their programs. The following sites offer extensive listings of camps throughout the United States.

Kids' Camps

http://www.kidscamps.com/

The Camp & Conference Homepage

http://www.camping.org/

InterCamp

http://www.Intercamp.com

Other Online Resources

Web sites are terrific sources of information on a variety of issues related to computers and gender equity. Many of the following sites also offer links to other relevant sites.

Camel Math

http://camel.math.ca/Women/EDU/Education.html

Educational issues for girls and women in mathematics published by the Canadian Mathematical Community (Camel).

Center for Media Education

http://tap.epn.org/cme

Produced ground-breaking report, *Web of Deception: Threats to Children from Online Marketing*, excerpts of which are available online.

Equity Online

http://www.edc.org/CEEC/womensequity

Equity Resource Center with many excellent materials for teachers.

Expect the Best From a Girl

http://www.academic.org

Suggestions and resources geared toward fostering self-confidence in girls and encouraging them in their pursuits. The site also has links to other online resources.

National Center for Missing and Exploited Children

http://www.missingkids.org/publications.html

The helpful brochure, "Child Safety On the Information Superhighway," is available at this site.

TAP Junior

http://www.cs.yale.edu/homes/tap/tap-junior.html

Information and links related to K–12 girls and computing.

Women and Technology, Harvard Graduate School of Education

http://gseweb.harvard.edu/TIEWeb/STUDENTS/
    STUDENTGROUPS/WIT/wit.html

A Harvard-based coalition to promote women and girls in technology. Site includes links to other online resources.

Books

Failing at Fairness: How America's Schools Cheat Girls

Myra and David Sadker

Charles Scribner's Sons: New York, 1994

An in-depth look at the unequal education received by girls and boys in the U.S.

The Internet Kids and Family Yellow Pages

Jean Armour Polly
Osborne/McGraw-Hill
2600 Tenth Street
Berkeley, CA 94710

An excellent family resource filled with fun and educational Web sites.

Lifting the Barriers

Jo Sanders
Washington Research Institute
150 Knickerson St. Suite 305
Seattle, WA 98109

This book offers strategies for parents and school personnel for encouraging girls' participation in math, science, and computer courses and activities.

The Neuter Computer

Jo Sanders and Antonia Stone
Neal-Schuman Publishers: New York. 1986.

Still one of the best resources for teachers on gender equity in computer use.

Notes

1. Quote taken from Ms. DeBold's comments at Microsoft Corporation's Equity in Technology Seminar, July 24, 1995.

2. As cited in, "America's Children and the Information Superhighway, An Update," Santa Monica: The Children's Partnership, 1996.

3. According to 1996 Bureau of Labor Statistics data, "systems analyst" and "computer engineers" are two of the five fastest-growing occupations.

4. American Association of University Women, *How Schools Shortchange Girls* (New York: Marlowe and Company, 1995), p. 47.

5. "American Learning Household Survey," New York: FIND/SVP in association with Grunwald Associates, 1995.

6. Northern Illinois University, Social Science Research Institute, special tabulations of the Longitudinal Study of American Youth, as cited in *Women, Minorities, and Persons with Disabilities in Science and Engineering.* (Arlington, VA: National Science Foundation, 1994).

7. William M. Buckeley, "Computers—The Gender Divide: A Tool for Women, a Toy for Men, Gender Affects How User Sees the Computer." *The Wall Street Journal,* 16 March 1994, B1.

8. *Ibid.*

9. R. Upitis, (in press). "From Hackers to Luddites, Game Players to Game Creators: Profiles of Adolescent Students Using Technology," *Journal of Curriculum Studies*.

10. "The Characteristics and Contributions of Home-Based Women-Owned Businesses in the U.S.," Silver Spring: The National Foundation for Women Business Owners, 1997.

11. *1996 Consumer End User Survey* (Washington, DC: Software Publishers Association).

12. "Web of Deception: Threats to Children from Online Marketing" (Washington, DC: Center for Media Education, 1996).

13. From "Assignment Incomplete: The Unfinished Business of Education Reform," New York: Public Agenda, 1995.

14. Thomas K. Glennan, and Arthur Melmed, "Fostering the Use of Educational Technology: Elements of a National Strategy," Washington, DC: RAND, 1996.

15. *Ibid.*

16. R. Upitis, and C. Koch, "Is Equal Computer Time Fair for Girls? Potential Internet Inequities." Proceedings of the 6th annual Conference of the Internet Society, INCT '96, Montreal, Quebec.

17. Myra and David Sadker, *Failing at Fairness: How America's Schools Cheat Girls* (New York: Charles Scribner's Sons, 1994), p. 42–44.

18. American Association of University Women Educational Foundation, "Growing Smart: What's Working for Girls in School" (Washington, DC: Executive Summary and Action Guide, 1995), p. 3.

19. Jo Sanders, "Girls and Technology Villain Wanted," in *Teaching the Majority: Breaking the Gender Barrier in Science, Mathematics, and Engineering*, ed. Sue V. Rosser (Teachers College Press, 1995).

20. American Association of University Women Educational Foundation, "Growing Smart: What's Working for Girls in School," pp. 17–19.

21. Sources: American Medical Association and the American Bar Association.

22. Statistics based on data compiled from the following sources: The National Center for Education Statistics; the U.S. Department of Education, Earned Degrees and Completion Surveys; Science Resources Studies Division, National Science Foundation; and the annual Taulbee Survey, conducted by the Computing Research Association.

23. The statistics are based on an analysis of profile data provided by seniors taking the SAT test in 1994, as reported in *Women, Minorities, and Persons with Disabilities in Science and Engineering* (Arlington, VA: National Science Foundation, 1996).

24. American Association of University Women, *Shortchanging Girls, Shortchanging America* (Washington, DC: *Executive Summary and Action Guide*, 1991).

25. National Science Foundation, *Women, Minorities, and Persons With Disabilities in Science and Engineering* (Arlington, VA: National Science Foundation, 1994).

26. Massachusetts Institute of Technology Department of Electrical Engineering and Computer Science, "Women Undergraduate Enrollment in Electrical Engineering and Computer Science at MIT" Final Report (Cambridge, MA: MIT Press, 1995).

27. Many additional tips and strategies can be found in *Lifting the Barriers*, by Jo Sanders, Port Washington: Jo Sanders Publications, 1994; and in *Girls and Technology*, a Resource Guide published by the National Coalition of Girls' Schools, Concord, Massachusetts.